THE SEVEN YEAR ITCH

 Random House, New York

The Seven Year Itch

A ROMANTIC COMEDY

BY GEORGE AXELROD

FOR GLORIA
AND
PETER AND STEVEN

The Seven Year Itch was first presented by Courtney Burr and Elliott Nugent at the Fulton Theatre on the evening of November 20, 1952, with the following cast:

RICHARD SHERMAN	*Tom Ewell*
RICKY	*Johnny Klein*
HELEN SHERMAN	*Neva Patterson*
MISS MORRIS	*Marilyn Clark*
ELAINE	*Joan Donovan*
MARIE WHATEVER-HER-NAME-WAS	*Irene Moore*
THE GIRL	*Vanessa Brown*
DR. BRUBAKER	*Robert Emhardt*
TOM MACKENZIE	*George Keane*
RICHARD'S VOICE	*George Ives*
THE GIRL'S VOICE	*Pat Fowler*

Directed by John Gerstad
Set and Lighting by Frederick Fox
Music composed and arranged by Dana Suesse
Production under the supervision of Elliott Nugent

SCENES

ACT ONE

Scene I—About eight o'clock on a summer evening.
Scene II—Immediately following.

ACT TWO

Scene I—Evening, the following day.
Scene II—Two hours later.

ACT THREE
The following morning

The action of the play takes place in the apartment of the Richard Shermans, in the Gramercy Park section of New York City.
The time is the present.

ACT ONE

ACT ONE

SCENE I

The apartment of the RICHARD SHERMANS, *about half a block from Gramercy Park in New York City.*

We see the foyer, the living room and the back terrace of a four-room apartment—the parlor floor through—in a re-modeled private house.

A flight of stairs on the back wall lead to the ceiling where they stop. In one of the earlier phases of remodeling, this apartment and the one above it were a duplex. But now they are rented separately and the ceiling is boarded up.

A door, also on the back wall, leads to the kitchen. French doors, right, open onto the terrace. The terrace, while it increases the rent about thirty dollars a month, is small and rather uninviting. It looks out into the back court and because of the buildings around it you get the feeling of being at the bottom of a well. From the terrace we see some of the skyline of the city and a good deal of the backs of the buildings across the court. On the terrace there is a chaise, a table and a few shrubs.

On the left wall of the living room are high, sliding doors which lead to the bedrooms and bath. There is a fireplace in the living room. The whole apartment has a summer look. The rugs are up and the summer slip covers are on the furniture. The living room contains a piano, bookshelves, a large radio phonograph and a liquor cabinet.

THE SEVEN YEAR ITCH

When the curtain rises it is about eight o'clock on an evening in July. It is a hot, airless night. It is not yet completely dark. It grows darker gradually through the scene.

RICHARD SHERMAN, *a young-looking man of thirty-eight, is lying on the chaise on the terrace. He wears a shirt, gabardine pants, loafers and no socks.*

It is hard to know what to say about RICHARD. *He has a crew haircut. He has a good job. He's vice-president in charge of sales at a twenty-five-cent publishing house. He made eighteen thousand dollars last year. He buys his clothes at Brooks.*

At the moment, he has moved a small, portable radio out to the table on the terrace and is listening to the first game of a twi-night double header between Brooklyn and Boston. He is listening to the game and drinking unenthusiastically from a bottle of Seven-Up.

At rise we hear the ball game softly on the radio. We have come in at a rather tense moment. The bases are loaded and Hodges is up. He bunts and is thrown out. RICHARD *is disgusted. He snaps off the radio.*

RICHARD
(*Rising*)

Bunt? Two runs behind, the bases loaded and they send Hodges up to bunt!

(*Shaking his head, he goes into the kitchen. He reappears carrying a bottle of raspberry soda. Still appalled*)

Bunt, for God's sake! Well, what are you going to do?

4

(*He looks around aimlessly for a moment*)

I'm hungry. Well, that's what comes of having dinner at Schrafft's! Schrafft's! I wanted to have dinner in the saloon across the street—but you can't have dinner in a saloon and then not . . . They don't like it. Oh, I suppose I could have ordered a drink and then not drunk it. . . . But I figure it's easier just to eat at Schrafft's.

(*He drops wearily onto the chaise*)

It's hard on a man when the family goes away. It's peaceful, though, with everybody gone. It's sure as hell peaceful.

(*He settles back in the chaise and grins. Music sneaks in very softly, and the light on him dims to a spot*)

Ricky was really upset this morning when they left for the station. It was very flattering. I thought the kid was going to cry. . . .

(*He sits, smiling, remembering the scene. Dream lighting by the front door picks up* HELEN *and* RICKY *leaving.*)

RICKY

But what about Daddy? Isn't Daddy coming with us?

HELEN

Daddy'll come up Friday night.

RICKY

But, Mommy, why can't Daddy come up with us now?

HELEN

Poor Daddy has to stay in the hot city and make money. We're going to spend the whole summer at the beach but poor Daddy can only come up week ends.

RICKY

Poor Daddy . . .

HELEN

Daddy is going to work very hard. He's going to eat properly and not smoke like Dr. Murphy told him and he's going to stay on the wagon for a while like Dr. Summers told him, to take care of his nervous indigestion. . . .

(*In the spot*, RICHARD *drinks from the bottle of raspberry soda. He is somewhat awed by the taste. He looks curiously at the label and then reads it.*)

RICHARD

"Contains carbonated water, citric acid, corn syrup, artificial raspberry flavoring, pure vegetable colors and preservative." Since I've been on the wagon, I've had one continuous upset stomach.

(*He looks sadly at the bottle and drinks some more.*)

6

HELEN

And just to make sure Daddy's all right, Mommy is going to call Daddy at ten o'clock tonight. . . .

RICKY

Poor Daddy . . .

(*The music fades and so does the dream light by the door.* HELEN *and* RICKY *disappear. The lighting returns to normal.*)

RICHARD
(*Coming out of his reverie*)

Ten o'clock! I don't even know how I'm going to stay awake till ten o'clock!

(*He stares moodily off into the growing dusk. Suddenly he notices something in an apartment across the court. He is momentarily fascinated and rises for a better look*)

Hey, lady! I know it's a hot night but . . . You sit out on this terrace, it's like having a television set with about thirty channels all going at once. . . . Don't give me any dirty look, lady. I pay rent for this terrace. If you don't like it, pull your blind down! (*As she apparently does so*) Oh. Well, that's life.

(*He yawns. Restlessly, he rises and wanders into the living room. He yawns again and then, suddenly, in mid-yawn, something occurs to him*)

Helen has a lot of nerve calling me at ten o'clock. It shows a very definite lack of trust.

What's she think I'm going to do? Start smoking the minute she turns her back? Start drinking? Maybe she thinks I'm going to have girls up here!

You know, that's a hell of a thing!

Seven years, we've been married. And not once have I done anything like that. Not *once*! And don't think I couldn't have, either. Because I could have. But plenty . . .

(*Music sneaks in and in dream lighting we see* HELEN *seated on the couch knitting. She laughs*)

Don't laugh. There're plenty of women who think I'm *pretty* attractive, for your information!

HELEN

For instance, who?

RICHARD
(*Indignant*)
What do you mean, for instance, who? There've been plenty of them, that's all.

HELEN

Name one.

(*There is a considerable pause while he thinks about this*)

Go ahead. Just one.

RICHARD

It's hard, I mean just offhand. There're plenty of them, though.

(HELEN *laughs.* RICHARD *is stung*)

Well, there's Miss Morris, for instance. She's practically thrown herself at me. You should see the way she gives me the business every time she comes into my office. . . .

(MISS MORRIS, *a sexy-looking blonde in a backless summer blouse and a skirt with an exaggerated slit, drifts into the scene carrying a dictation pad and pencil*)

She wears those backless things and she's always telling me it's so hot she's not wearing any underwear. . . .

HELEN

It sounds perfectly sordid. Does she sit on your lap when she takes dictation?

RICHARD

Of course not!

(MISS MORRIS *sits on his lap.*)

MISS MORRIS

Good morning, Mr. Sherman.

9

RICHARD

Good morning, Miss Morris.

(MISS MORRIS *runs her fingers through his hair and covers his cheek and neck with little kisses*)

That will be all.

(MISS MORRIS *gets up and drifts away, giving him a private wave and a wink*)

I just happened to bring her up as an example, that's all. Just an example . . .

HELEN

I'm quite sure you're a great success with the stenographers in your office.

RICHARD

I could be a great success with a couple of your high-class friends if you're going to get snooty about it. Elaine, for instance. You may not know this, but for *two years* that dame has been trying to get me into the sack. . . .

(ELAINE, *a luscious-looking dame in a gold-lamé evening gown, appears on the terrace. She is carrying a glass of champagne*)

The night of your birthday party, she got loaded and went after me right here on the terrace. . . .

(*Dream lighting on Helen dims out.*)

ELAINE

(*Coming up behind him and draping her arms around his neck*)

Do you know something, darling? I look at you and I just melt. You must know that. Men always know...

(*Quite casually she tosses her champagne glass off the terrace and grabs him and kisses him violently.*)

RICHARD

What's the matter? Are you crazy or something?

ELAINE

Let's get out of here, darling. Come on. Nobody'll even know we're gone....

RICHARD

You don't know what you're sayir g!

ELAINE

Oh, yes, I do! Come on, darling! Let's be a little mad!

(*She drifts away, giving him the eye as she goes.*)

RICHARD

Now, Elaine may be a little mad, but she's plenty attractive! And *she's* not the only one either! You probably don't even remember that Marie whatever-her-name-was, from the UN who was staying with the Petersons in Westport last summer....

We went swimming together one night. Without any bathing suits. You didn't know that, did you? It was that Saturday night the MacKenzies came up and I drove over to the beach by myself ...

(MARIE WHATEVER-HER-NAME-WAS *has materialized beside him. A gorgeous girl in shorts and man's shirt.*)

MARIE
(*Speaking in rapid but somehow sexy-sounding French*)
Hello, Dick. You too, without doubt, like to swim at night. I like it because the wearing of a bathing suit is unnecessary. . . .

(*She kicks off her shorts and as she talks begins to unbutton her shirt*)

RICHARD
I don't speak very good French, but I knew what she was talking about.

MARIE
The water at night is magnificent. There is a warmness and a feeling of black velvet. Especially when one is without bathing costume ...

RICHARD
(*Weakly, unable to take his eyes off the buttons*)
Mais oui. Mais oui.

MARIE

Voilà! Let us go!

(Her shirt is almost off. The lights dim out just in time.)

RICHARD
(With great self-righteousness)
We didn't do anything but swim. As a matter of fact, she was plenty disappointed we didn't do anything but swim.

(The lights have dimmed back to normal)

So, all I can say is, in the light of the circumstances, I resent your calling me at ten o'clock to check up on me. If Helen is going to start worrying about me after seven years, it's pretty ridiculous, that's all.

(He rises and begins to pace nervously)

And she is worried too. Even if she doesn't show it. I don't know. She probably figures she isn't as young as she used to be. She's thirty-one years old. One of these days she's going to wake up and find her looks are gone. Then where will she be? No wonder she's worried.

Especially since I don't look a bit different than I did when I was twenty-eight.

It's not my fault I don't. It's just a simple biological fact. Women age quicker than men. I probably won't look any different when I'm sixty. I have that kind of a face. Everybody'll think she's my mother.

13

(*He sighs a mournful sigh and sinks into chair. The downstairs door buzzer rings*)

Now who's that? (*He goes to the foyer and presses the wall button. Then he opens the front door and peers out calling*)
Hello? Hello? Who is it?

GIRL'S VOICE
(*Off stage*)
I'm terribly sorry to bother you ...

RICHARD
What?
(*Then as he sees her, he reacts*)
Oh. Oh. Well, hello ...

GIRL'S VOICE
(*Off stage*)
I feel so silly. I forgot my key. I locked myself out. So I pressed your bell. I hope you don't mind.

RICHARD
No. No. I don't mind. No trouble at all.

GIRL'S VOICE
(*Off stage*)
I'm awfully sorry.

RICHARD

Don't worry about it. Any time. It's a pleasure.

GIRL'S VOICE
(*Off stage*)

Thank you. Well, good-bye . . .

RICHARD

Good-bye . . .

(*He closes the door. Then, after a moment opens it again and peers out, craning his neck to see up the stairs. He comes back inside, closes the door. He is shaking his head.*)

RICHARD

Where did *that* come from? I didn't know they made them like that any more. Oh, she must be the one who sublet the Kaufmans' apartment. I should have asked her in for a drink. Oh, no, I shouldn't have. Not me, kid.

(*The telephone rings.* RICHARD *glances at his watch. Then hurries to answer it*)

Hello? Oh. Hello, Helen. I wasn't expecting you to call till ten. Is everything okay? . . . Good. . . . I was just sitting here listening to the ball game. They're two runs behind and they send Hodges up to bunt. . . . Yeah, I'm sleepy too. . . . The old place is pretty empty without you. I can't wait till Friday. Ricky okay? . . . He did? Well, he hasn't done that for a long time. It was probably just the excitement. . . .

That's nice. No, I don't. . . . Who did you meet at the A & P?

What's Tom MacKenzie doing up there? . . . Look, my advice to you is avoid Tom MacKenzie like the plague. If you keep meeting him at the A&P, switch to Bohack's!

Look, are you sure everything else is all right? Good. . . . Me too. Yeah, I'm pretty tired myself. Good night. . . . Night.

(*He hangs up phone*)

Well, I might as well go to sleep myself. But I'm not sleepy. I suddenly realize I am not even a little bit sleepy. Maybe I could call up Charlie Peterson. No. That's a real bad idea. Under no circumstances should I call up Charlie Peterson.

I'll get in bed and read. God knows I've got enough stuff here I'm supposed to read.

(*Picks up brief case and begins to take out manuscripts*)

I've got a conference with Dr. Brubaker tomorrow night. It might be amusing if I'd finished his miserable book before I talk to him about it. I don't know why every psychiatrist in America feels he has to write a book. And let's see what else. *The Scarlet Letter.* I read that in school. I don't have to read that again. But I'd better. Dr. Brubaker and *The Scarlet Letter.* It looks like a big night. (*Picks up soda bottle, notices that it is empty*) Well, one more of these for a night cap and we're all set. . . .

(*Sighing heavily, he goes to kitchen for a fresh bottle of soda. He walks back out to the terrace and sits for a moment on the chaise. Automatically, he switches on the radio.*)

RADIO VOICE

. . . and so as we go into the last half of the eighth inning, Boston is leading, seven to four. In the last of the eighth, for Brooklyn, it'll be Robinson, Hodges and Furillo . . .

(RICHARD *reaches over and snaps off the radio.*)

RICHARD

Frankly, I don't give a damn.

(*He rises and walks to the edge of the terrace, looking hopefully toward the apartment across the court.*)
(*At that moment there is a violent crash. Apparently from the sky, an enormous iron pot with a plant in it comes plummeting down. It lands with a sickening thud on the chaise where he was sitting a moment before.*)
(RICHARD *looks at it in horror-struck silence for a moment or two.*)

RICHARD

Look at that damn thing! Right where I was sitting! I could have been killed, for God's sake!

(*Cautiously, with a nervous glance upward, he leans over to examine it*)

Jes-sus!

(*He darts back inside, looks wildly around for a cigarette, finally finds a crumbled pack in the pocket of a raincoat hanging in the hall closet. He starts to light it. Then, stops himself*)

I forgot—I'm not smoking. Oh, the hell with *that*!

(*He lights the cigarette*)

I could have been killed. Just then. Like that. Right now I could be lying out there on the lousy terrace dead. I should stop smoking because twenty years from now it might affect my goddamn lungs!

(*He inhales deeply with great enjoyment*)

Oh, that tastes beautiful. The first one in six weeks.

(*He lets the smoke out slowly*)

All those lovely injurious tars and resins!

(*Suddenly he is dizzy*)

I'm dizzy. . . .

(*He sinks to the piano bench, coughing*)

Another week of not smoking and I'd really've been dead!

(*He picks up the bottle of soda and starts to take a slug of that. He chokes on it*)

The hell with this stuff too!

(*He goes quickly to liquor cabinet and pours an inch or two of whiskey into a glass and belts it down. Then he mixes another one and carries it onto the terrace. He sets the drink on the table and in a very gingerly fashion tries to pick up the pot. It is real heavy*)

My God! This thing weighs a ton! I could have been killed!

(*Suddenly, his anger finds a direction*)

Hey, up there! What's the big idea! You want to kill somebody or something? What do you think you're doing anyway?

GIRL'S VOICE
(*From terrace above*)
What's the matter?

RICHARD
(*Yelling*)
What's the matter? This goddamn cast-iron chamber pot damn near killed me, that's what's the matter. What the hell! ... Oh. Oh. It's you. Hello.

GIRL'S VOICE
What hap——Oh, golly! The tomato plant fell over?

RICHARD
It sure did.

GIRL'S VOICE
I'm terribly sorry.

RICHARD
That's okay.

GIRL'S VOICE
I seem to be giving you a terrible time tonight. First the door and now this. I don't know what to do. . . .

RICHARD
Don't worry about it. (*He drains drink*) Hey, up there!

GIRL'S VOICE
Yes?

RICHARD
I'll tell you what you can do about it. You can come down and have a drink.

GIRL'S VOICE
But that doesn't seem . . .

RICHARD
Sure it seems . . . Come on now . . . I insist . . .

GIRL'S VOICE
Well, all right . . .

RICHARD
I'll see you in a minute.

GIRL'S VOICE
All right. I'm really terribly sorry. . . .
That's okay. Don't worry about it. As a matter of fact, it's
wonderful. See you in a minute . . .

GIRL'S VOICE
All right . . .

(RICHARD *gallops frantically into the living room.
The sound of the telephone brings him up short. He
goes quickly to phone and answers it.*)

RICHARD
Hi there! Oh. Oh, Helen!

(*With great, if somewhat forced enthusiasm.*)

Well, Helen! This *is* a surprise! And a very pleasant one
if I may say so! How *are you?*
Sure, sure I'm all right. Why shouldn't I be all right? In
what way do I sound funny? I was just out on the terrace
listening to the ball game. They're two runs behind and they
send Hodges up to bunt. . . . What? Sure . . . Sure I will.
Your yellow skirt . . .

(*As she talks on the other end of the phone he is
reaching around straightening up the room*)

21

Yes, of course I'm listening to you. You want me to send up your yellow skirt, because you're having Tom MacKenzie and some people over for cocktails. Good old Tom! How is he?

No. I haven't been drinking. I just had . . . What? Your yellow skirt. In the hall closet. On a wire hanger. Sure. By parcel post. The first thing in the morning. Without fail.

No. I don't feel a bit funny. I was just out on the terrace listening to the ball game. They're two runs behind and they send Hodges up . . . Yes . . . well, good night. Good night. Night.

> (*He hangs up phone. Then, galvanized into action, he starts to straighten up the place. In the middle of this he realizes he looks a little sloppy himself and he dashes off through the bedroom doors. Music swells and the lights dim out.*)

Curtain

ACT ONE

SCENE II

The music continues through the blackout.
After a moment the curtain rises and the lights dim back up to normal.

RICHARD *reappears from the bedroom. He has put on the jacket to his pants and is frantically tying his tie.*

He is visibly agitated. He starts to arrange the room for his guest. He pauses and turns off a lamp. Catches himself and quickly turns it back on again.

RICHARD

What am I *doing* anyway!

This is absolutely ridiculous. The first night Helen leaves and I'm bringing dames into the apartment.

Now take it easy. The girl upstairs damn near kills me with a cast-iron bucket. So I ask her down for a drink. What's wrong with that?

If Helen was here, she'd do the same thing. It's only polite.

And what the hell is she doing asking Tom MacKenzie over for cocktails, for God's sake!

Besides, I want to get another look at that girl. She must be some kind of a model or actress or something.

(*He is busily arranging things. Laying out ice and soda. Puffing cushions. Picking up his socks*)

There is absolutely nothing wrong with asking a neighbor down for a drink. Nothing.

I just hope *she* doesn't get the wrong idea, that's all. If this dame thinks she's coming down here for some kind of a big time or something—well, she's got a big surprise. One drink and out! That's all! I'm a happily married man, for God's sake!

(*He surveys his work*)

Maybe we ought to have a little soft music, just for atmossphere.

(*He goes to phonograph and starts looking through records*)

Let's see. How about the Second Piano Concerto? Maybe Rachmaninoff would be overdoing it a little. This kid is probably more for old show tunes. . . .

(*He finds a record: "Just One of Those Things"—it is obviously an old one with a real thirties orchestration. He puts it on and listens to it for a moment or two with great satisfaction*)

That's more like it. The old nostalgia. Never misses. . . . *Never misses? What am I trying to do?* I'll call her and tell her not to come. That's all. Why ask for trouble?

(*He starts for phone—stops*)

I don't even know her phone number. I don't even know her name. What am I doing? And what the hell is she doing?

She could have been down here, had her lousy drink, and gone home already!

She's probably getting all fixed up. She'll probably be wearing some kind of a damn evening dress!

Oh, my God! What have I done?

(*Very quickly he has another drink*)

If anything happens, it happens. That's all. It's up to her. She looked kind of sophisticated. She must know what she's doing.

I'm pretty sophisticated myself. At least I used to be. I've been married so damn long I don't remember.

(*Suddenly, he becomes very polished.*)

Drink?

Thanks.

(*He pours himself a drink*)

Soda?

A dash.

(*He toasts*)

Cheers.

(*He leans nonchalantly against the piano. The "real" lighting begins to dim and music: "Just One of Those Things" fades in. The front door lights up and swings*)

25

majestically open flooding the room with "dream light". He moves toward the door, almost dancing. In this particular flight of fancy he is very suave, very Noel Coward.)

(The GIRL *is standing in the doorway. She is an extraordinarily beautiful girl in her early twenties. She wears an extravagantly glamorous evening gown. There is a wise, half-mocking, half-enticing smile on her face. She looks like nothing so much as a Tabu perfume ad.)*

THE GIRL

I came.

RICHARD

I'm so glad.

THE GIRL

Didn't you know I'd come?

RICHARD

Of course. Of course I knew. Won't you come in?

THE GIRL

Thank you.

(She comes in. The door swings closed behind her.)
(RICHARD turns and we suddenly notice that he is wearing a black patch over one eye.)

26

RICHARD

How lovely you are! Tell me, who are you? What is your name?

THE GIRL

Does it matter?

RICHARD

No. Of course not. I was a boor to ask.

THE GIRL

Why have you invited me here?

RICHARD

(*Spoken—like dialogue*)

Oh, it was just one of those things. Just one of those foolish things. A trip to the moon—on gossamer wings ...

THE GIRL

How sweet! Oh—a Steinway. Do you play?

RICHARD

(*Somewhat wistfully. Thinking, perhaps, of other, happier days*)

Just a little now—for myself ...

THE GIRL

Play something for me. ...

THE SEVEN YEAR ITCH

RICHARD

All right. You'll be sorry you asked. . . .

THE GIRL

I'm sure I'll not . . .

RICHARD

(*Sitting at piano*)

You'll see . . .

(*Very dramatically he prepares to play. His preparations, while vastly complicated, do not, however, include raising the lid from the keys. Finally he begins to play—or rather pantomime playing on the closed lid. We hear, however, the opening bars of the C Sharp Minor Prelude played brilliantly.*)

RICHARD

(*Playing*)

I'm afraid I'm a little rusty.

(*She is overcome. She sinks to the piano bench beside him. He turns to her*)

Tell me, what would you think, if, quite suddenly, I were to seize you in my arms and cover your neck with kisses?

THE GIRL

I would think: What a mad impetuous fool he is!

28

RICHARD

And if I merely continued to sit here, mooning at you, as I have done for the last half hour—what would you think then?

THE GIRL

I would simply think: What a fool he is!

(RICHARD *takes her dramatically in his arms. They embrace. He kisses her violently. Music sweeps in and the lights black out.*)

(*In the darkness, we hear the sound of the door buzzer. It rings twice.*)

(*The lights dim back to normal.* RICHARD *is standing where we left him, leaning against the piano, lost in reverie. The buzzer rings again and he is jarred back to reality. He puts down his drink, and falling all over himself in nervous and undignified haste dashes to the door*)

RICHARD

Come in . . . Come in . . .

(*Revealed in the doorway is* DR. BRUBAKER. *He is a round, somewhat messy, imperious man in his middle fifties. He carries a large brief case.*)

RICHARD
(*Completely taken aback*)

Dr. Brubaker!

DR. BRUBAKER

Good evening. I hope I'm not late. Monday is my day at the clinic plus my regular patients and of course I'm on The Author Meets the Critic Friday night. I have been preparing my denunciation. I hope I haven't kept you waiting. . . .

RICHARD

Look, Dr. Brubaker. Wasn't our. . . ?

DR. BRUBAKER

Your office sent me the galleys of the last five chapters. I have them here with me. They are a mass of errors. I want to go over the whole thing with you very carefully.

RICHARD

Dr. Brubaker. I'm terribly sorry. Our appointment—I believe it was for tomorrow night. . . .

(DR. BRUBAKER *has opened his brief case and has begun to spread papers all over the table.*)

DR. BRUBAKER

I understand, of course, that your firm wishes to reach as wide an audience as possible. But I must protest—and very strongly—the changing of the title of my book from *Of Man and the Unconscious* to *Of Sex and Violence.* . . .

RICHARD

Dr. Brubaker, I'm terribly sorry. I know how important this is. But I'm afraid our appointment was for tomorrow night.

DR. BRUBAKER

Tomorrow night?

RICHARD

Tuesday night. I understood it was definite for Tuesday night.

DR. BRUBAKER

Good Lord!

RICHARD

And I'm afraid I have someone coming in tonight. Another appointment. With an author. And she'll be here any minute. In fact she's late.

DR. BRUBAKER

Astounding. Really incredible.

RICHARD

It's probably my fault. I probably wasn't clear on the phone.

DR. BRUBAKER

No. No. You were perfectly clear. . . .

RICHARD

I can't understand how it happened.

DR. BRUBAKER

Perfectly simple. Repressed uxoricide.

RICHARD

I beg your pardon?

DR. BRUBAKER

Repressed uxoricide. I came tonight because I want to murder my wife.

RICHARD

I see. . . . Yes . . . Of course . . .

DR. BRUBAKER

A perfectly natural phenomenon. It happens every day.

RICHARD

It does?

DR. BRUBAKER

Certainly. Upon leaving the clinic and being faced with the necessity of returning to my home, I felt a strong unconscious impulse to murder my wife. Naturally, not wanting to do the good woman any bodily harm, my mind conveniently changed our appointment to tonight. What could be more simple?

RICHARD

I see. . . .

THE SEVEN YEAR ITCH

DR. BRUBAKER
I am most sorry to have inconvenienced you, sir. . . .

RICHARD
No, no. That's quite all right. . . .

DR. BRUBAKER
And I shall see you here tomorrow evening.

RICHARD
Fine, Doctor. We could just as easily have our conference tonight—except that I do have this other author coming. . . .

DR. BRUBAKER
Of course. I understand perfectly. Oh . . . Have you finished reading the book?

RICHARD
Well, I got as far as Chapter Three. The Meyerholt Case.

DR. BRUBAKER
Meyer*heim.* You read very slowly. Well, sir. Good night.

(*He turns and starts to go. He is almost to the door when he stops and turns back*)

Sir. I trust you will not be offended if I call to your attention the fact that you are not wearing socks. . . .

RICHARD
(*Looking down*)

Good Lord!

DR. BRUBAKER

I was interested in knowing if you were aware of it? And I gather from your expression that you were not. In Chapter Three on Gustav Meyerheim I point out that he invariably removed his socks. Before he struck.

RICHARD

Before—he *struck*?

DR. BRUBAKER

Yes. Surely you recall Meyerheim. A fascinating character! A rapist! I was certain you would be amused by the coincidence. Until tomorrow then, good evening.

(*The* DOCTOR *bows and exits.*)

(RICHARD *looks helplessly down at his sockless ankles, then looks wildly around, finds his socks and struggles into them, muttering angrily as he does so something that sounds vaguely like: "Damn psychiatrists—write books—make a Federal case out of everything. . . . I bet his wife is a nervous wreck—every time he takes off his socks she probably hides in the closet. . . ."*)

(*As he is fighting his way into his loafers the door buzzer sounds.*)

34

RICHARD

Coming ...

(*He dashes to door and opens it.* THE GIRL *is standing in the doorway. Her real-life entrance is very different from the way he imagined it. She is quite lovely but far from the exotic creature he envisioned. She wears a checked shirt and rolled dungarees. She looks at him for a moment and then smiles tentatively.*)

THE GIRL

Hi.

RICHARD

(*He looks at her blankly for an instant*)

Hi.

THE GIRL

Can I come in?

RICHARD

Sure ... I mean, of course. Please do.

THE GIRL

I'm sorry I took so long but I've been watering the garden. I promised the Kaufmans I'd take good care of it, and I'm afraid I kind of neglected it. I didn't even find the hose until tonight.

RICHARD

I didn't know the Kaufmans had a garden. ...

THE GIRL

Oh, yes. They do.

RICHARD

It must be very nice.

THE GIRL

It is. But it's a lot of work. Before I found the hose I'd been using the cocktail shaker—that was the only thing I could find. . . .

RICHARD

The cocktail shaker . . .

THE GIRL

Yes. They have a big glass one. It must hold about a gallon. I'm just sick about the tomato plant. Did it survive, do you think?

RICHARD

I really don't know. We could look at it, I suppose. It's out on the terrace. Right where it landed.

THE GIRL

That's awful. . . . I can't figure out how it happened. . . .

(RICHARD *leads way to terrace.*)

RICHARD

It's right there. I haven't touched it. . . .

THE GIRL

Golly, look at that! I'll pay for it, of course. Do you think you could lift it up...?

RICHARD

Sure.
> (*He lifts the pot off the chaise with a great deal of effort*)

This damn thing weighs a ton.... There ..

THE GIRL

I just thought. If you'd been sitting in that chair ... When it fell, I mean. It might have, well—practically killed you....

RICHARD

That occurred to me, too.

THE GIRL

I'm really awfully sorry. It's probably criminal negligence or manslaughter or something. You could have sued somebody. Me, probably. Or your family could have. Of course I don't know what they would have collected. If they'd sued me, I mean. But anyway, they'd have had a very good case.

RICHARD

There's no use getting all upset. I wasn't sitting there, thank God, so it's all right. Look, I asked you down for a drink. Would you like one? I mean you really don't look old enough to drink....

THE GIRL

I do, though. I drink like a fish. Do you have Scotch?

RICHARD

Sure. At least I'm pretty sure I do. I've been drinking some-thing for the last half hour. I'm not sure now what it was. I was a little upset. . . .

THE GIRL

(*Following him back into the living room*)
I don't blame you. You could have been killed, practically. I feel just terrible about it. I mean . . .

RICHARD

Let's don't start that again. Let's just have a drink.

THE GIRL

All right. I'm glad you're taking it this way. You have every right to be just furious. I know I would be. If somebody prac-tically dropped a tomato plant on my head.

RICHARD

Let's see, what I *was* drinking?

(*Picks up glass and tastes it*)

Bourbon. But we do have Scotch around here somewhere. Yeah—here we are. How do you like it?

38

THE GIRL

Scotch and soda, I guess. That's what you're supposed to say, isn't it? Back home the boys drink Scotch and Pepsi-Cola a lot. Before I knew anything at all, I knew *that* was wrong.

RICHARD

That's about as wrong as you can get, yes.

THE GIRL

I knew it was. When I was very young I liked it, though. It sort of killed the taste of the Scotch.

RICHARD
(*Mixing drink*)

I can see how it would tend to do that.

THE GIRL

Do you have a cigarette around? I left mine upstairs.

RICHARD

Oh, yes. Sure. I'm sorry. Right here.
(*He takes the crumpled pack from his pocket. There is one left in it*)

It may be a little stale. I haven't been smoking. In fact, before tonight, I hadn't had a cigarette in six weeks.

THE GIRL

That's wonderful! I wish I had the will power to stop. I don't, though. I smoke like a chimney. Sometimes three packs a day.

RICHARD

My God! That's terrifying.

THE GIRL

I know. It doesn't seem to affect me, though. I guess I'm pretty healthy. What made you start aga—— Oh. I'll bet you started smoking after the plant fell down. To steady your nerves.

RICHARD

Well, something like that.

THE GIRL

Now I really *do* feel awful. If I'd just had the sense to move it off the wall. Or call the janitor and have him move it. It's pretty heavy. . . . Oh, I just feel . . .

RICHARD

Please, now, that's enough. Let me get some more cigarettes. I think there's an unopened carton out in the kitchen. Excuse me a minute. . . .

(*He exits into the kitchen.*)

(*The* GIRL *looks around the apartment then drifts over to the piano. She hits a random note or two.* RICHARD *reappears.*)

THE GIRL

Do you play the piano?

40

(*For one mad instant,* RICHARD *considers the question. The faraway "Just-a-little-now-for-myself" look comes into his eye. But he quickly suppresses it.*)

RICHARD
(*Truthfully*)
I'm afraid not. I'm tone deaf. My wife plays, though. . . .

THE GIRL
Oh, you're married?

RICHARD
Yes. I am.

THE GIRL
I knew it! I could tell. You *look* married.

RICHARD
I do?

THE GIRL
Mmm! It's funny. Back home practically nobody was married. And in New York everybody is. Men, I mean.

RICHARD
That's a remarkable observation.

THE GIRL
It's really true.

RICHARD

I guess so. I never really thought about it.

THE GIRL

(*As he hands her drink*)

Thanks. I think about it quite a lot. This is good. Do you mind if I put my feet up. I'll take my shoes off.

RICHARD

No. Of course not. Go right ahead. Make yourself comfortable.

THE GIRL

Your wife is away for the summer, isn't she?

RICHARD

Yes, as a matter of fact she is. How did you know?

THE GIRL

They all are. It's really amazing.

RICHARD

They *all* are?

THE GIRL

Mmm. Everybody's wife. Back home practically nobody goes away for the summer. Especially anybody's wife.

RICHARD

Have you been away long? In New York, that is?

THE GIRL

Oh, years. Almost a year and a half. It seems like years.
I love it. Especially now that I've got my own apartment.
When I lived at the club I didn't like it so much. You had
to be in by one o'clock. Now I can stay out all night if I want
to. I was really glad when they practically asked me to leave.

RICHARD

Why did they practically ask you to leave?

THE GIRL

It was so silly. I used to do modeling when I first came to
New York and when this picture of me was published in *US
Camera* they got all upset. You should have seen Miss Ste-
phenson's face. She was the house mother.

RICHARD

What was the matter with the picture?

THE GIRL

I was nude.

RICHARD

Oh.

THE GIRL

On the beach with some driftwood. It got honorable mention. It was called "Textures". Because you could see the three
different textures. The driftwood, the sand and me. I got

twenty-five dollars an hour. And it took hours and hours, you'd be surprised. And the first day the sun wasn't right and I got paid for that too.

RICHARD

That seems only fair.

THE GIRL

Sure. You get paid from the time you're called. No matter how long it takes to make the picture. But I don't do modeling any more. Since I got this steady job ...

RICHARD

Now you have a steady job?

THE GIRL

I take in washing. . . .

RICHARD

What?

THE GIRL

That's just a joke. I'm on this television program. The commercial part. First I wash my husband's shirt in *ordinary* soap flakes. Then I wash it with Trill. So when people ask me what I do I always say I take in washing. I'm on for a minute and forty-five seconds. It's really a very good part. . . .

RICHARD

Oh, so you're an actress. Is that it?

THE GIRL

Mmm. It's really very interesting. People don't realize, but every time I wash a shirt on television, I'm appearing before more people than Sarah Bernhardt appeared before in her whole career. It's something to think about.

RICHARD

It certainly is.

THE GIRL

I wish *I* were old enough to have seen Sarah Bernhardt. Was she magnificent?

> (RICHARD *is somewhat shaken by this question. For a moment he sits there, grinning weakly.*)

RICHARD

I really wouldn't know. I'm not quite that old myself. . . .

THE GIRL

I guess you're really not, are you?

RICHARD

I am thirty-nine. Or I will be the day after tomorrow. At the moment I'm still only thirty-eight.

THE GIRL

The day after tomorrow?

RICHARD

That's right.

THE GIRL

Isn't that amazing? We were born under the same sign. I was twenty-two yesterday. I didn't do anything about it, though. I didn't even tell anyone. Oh, I did one thing. I bought a bottle of champagne. I thought I'd sit there and drink it all by myself. . . .

RICHARD

That sounds absolutely sad . . .

THE GIRL

Oh, no. It would have been fun. Sitting in my own apartment drinking champagne. But I couldn't get the bottle open. You're not supposed to use a corkscrew. You're supposed to work the cork loose with your thumbs. I just couldn't seem to do it. I suppose I could have called the janitor or something. But, somehow, I didn't feel like calling the janitor to open a bottle of champagne on my birthday. Look, I got blisters on both thumbs. Well, not really blisters, but I sort of pulled the thumb part away from the nail . . .

RICHARD

It's not really a matter of brute force. It's more of a trick. (*Demonstrating with thumbs*) You kind of get one side and then the other and it finally works loose. . . . You have to have strong thumbs, though. . . .

THE GIRL

I've got a wonderful idea. Let me go up and get it. It's just sitting there in the ice box. We could both drink it. Since we both have birthdays. If you can really get it open . . .

RICHARD

I'm pretty sure I could get it open—but I don't want to drink your . . .

THE GIRL

It would be fun. After I couldn't get it open I sort of lost interest in sitting up there and drinking it alone. Let me go up and get it and we'll have a double birthday party. It's very good champagne. The man said.

RICHARD

I don't really think . . .

THE GIRL

I told him to be sure and give me very good champagne. Because I couldn't tell the difference myself. Wouldn't you like to?

RICHARD

Sure. As a matter of fact, I'd love to. I think we've got some champagne glasses in the kitchen . . .

THE GIRL

Okay. I'll go up and get it. I'll be right back. Should I bring the potato chips too?

RICHARD

Sure. Let's shoot the works!

THE GIRL

That's just the way I felt. I'll be right back.

RICHARD

Okay.

THE GIRL

See you in a minute . . .

(She exits, closing the door behind her.)

(RICHARD stares after her, somewhat bewildered. He picks up his glass, drains it, shakes his head, picks up her glass and starts toward the kitchen. Suddenly, he stops and turns back, a reflective expression on his face.)

RICHARD

US Camera . . .

(He puts down the glasses and goes to the bookshelf. He looks for a moment and then finds what he is looking for. He takes down a book. It is a very large book, very clearly marked: US Camera. *He begins, in a casual way, to riffle through the pages.)*

(Muttering)

News events . . . Children and Animals . . . The Human Body . . .

(He turns the pages slowly and then suddenly stops. He stares. He closes the book, puts it back on the shelf, picks up the glasses and goes swiftly into the kitchen. After a moment he comes back again, carrying two champagne glasses. He polishes them, sets them down, starts for the book and stops himself. Instead he pours a little whiskey into one of the champagne glasses,

*gulps it down, then wipes it out with his handkerchief.
Finally he pulls himself together*)

Let's see . . . Birthday party!

(*He starts to fix things up a little bit. Goes to phonograph and looks through records*)

Show tunes . . .

(*He puts on a record: "Falling in Love with Love"*)

In seven years I never did anything like this! In another
seven years I won't be able to.

(*On this sobering thought, he sits down and stares
moodily into space—the music from the record fades
softly down.*)

HIS VOICE

Hey, Dick. Dickie boy . . .

RICHARD

Yeah, Richard?

HIS VOICE

What do you think you're doing?

RICHARD

I don't know. I don't know what I'm doing.

HIS VOICE

This kid is just a little young, don't you think?

RICHARD

Look, let me alone, will you?

HIS VOICE

Okay. You know what you're doing.

RICHARD

No, I don't. I really don't.

HIS VOICE

Relax. You're not doing anything. Even if you wanted to
—you haven't got a chance. . . .

RICHARD

Oh yeah? That's what you think. She seems to like me.
She seems kind of fascinated by me.

HIS VOICE

She thinks you're that nice Sarah Bernhardt fan who lives
downstairs. You're getting older, boy. You got bags under
your eyes. You're getting fat.

RICHARD

Fat? Where?

HIS VOICE

Under your chin there. You're getting a martini pouch. And
that crew-cut stuff! You're not kidding anybody. One of these
mornings you're going to look in the mirror and that's all,
brother. The Portrait of Dorian Gray.

(RICHARD *examines himself nervously in the mirror.*
He is only slightly reassured.)

RICHARD
Look, pal, I'm going to level with you. This is a real pretty
girl—and, as we pointed out, I'm not getting any younger—
so . . .

HIS VOICE
Okay, pal. You're on your own . . .

(*He stands there for a moment of nervous indecision.*
The buzzer sounds. He decides—and with a new
briskness in his step heads gaily for the door. He opens
the door, admitting the girl. She comes in. She has
changed to a sophisticated cocktail dress. She carries
champagne and a bag of potato chips.)

THE GIRL
Hi. I'm sorry I took so long. I thought I ought to change.
I got this dress at Ohrbach's. But I don't think you could tell,
could you?

RICHARD
You look lovely.
(*She reacts slightly, sensing a difference in his tone.*)

THE GIRL
Thank you. Here's the champagne. You can see where I
was working on it. . . .

RICHARD

Let me take a crack at it. (*He takes bottle and begins to thumb cork*) This is a tough one....

THE GIRL

Should I do anything?

RICHARD

I don't think so. Just stand well back...

(*He struggles with cork.*)

THE GIRL

We could call the janitor. He's probably got some kind of an instrument...

RICHARD

(*Through clenched teeth as he struggles*)
No—let's—keep—the janitor out of this.... Damn it...
This thing is in here like...

THE GIRL

I told you. You can just imagine what I went through. On my birthday and everything.

RICHARD

(*He stops to rest*)
You know, this is just a lot of damn chi-chi nonsense. They could put a regular cork in this stuff and you could just pull it with a corkscrew....

(*He attacks it again*)

Come on, you stinker!

Hey—I think—watch out—maybe you better get a glass just in case she . . .

>   (*The cork finally pops*)

Catch it! Catch it!

>   (*She catches it.*)

THE GIRL

Got it! Boy, you sure have powerful thumbs. . . .

RICHARD

>   (*He is rather pleased by this*)

I used to play a lot of tennis. . . .

THE GIRL

Do you think it's cold enough? I just had it sitting in the ice box. . . .

RICHARD

It's fine. . . . Well, happy birthday.

THE GIRL

Happy birthday. (*They touch glasses and drink*) Is it all right? I mean is that how it's supposed to taste. . . ?

RICHARD

That's how.

>   (*She takes another tentative taste.*)

THE GIRL

You know, it's pretty good. I was sort of afraid it would taste like Seven-Up or something. . . .

RICHARD

Hey, I forgot . . .

(*He leans forward and plants a quick, nervous kiss on her forehead*)

Birthday kiss. Happy birthday.

THE GIRL

Thank you. Same to you.

RICHARD

Maybe we ought to have some music or something. Since this is a party . . .

THE GIRL

That's a good idea. . . .

RICHARD

I've got about a million records here. We can probably find something appropriate. Ready for some more?

THE GIRL

Not quite yet.

(*He refills his own glass.*)

THE GIRL

I've kind of stopped buying records. I mean I didn't have a machine for so long. Now that I've got one again—or anyway the Kaufmans have one—I'm all out of the habit. . . .

RICHARD

Do you like show tunes?

THE GIRL

Sure. Do you have "The King and I"?

RICHARD

I'm afraid I don't. That's a little recent for me. I've got mostly old Rodgers and Hart and Cole Porter and Gershwin. . . . How about this one? From "Knickerbocker Holiday."

(He is offering a prized possession: The Walter Huston recording of "September Song." He puts it on and they listen for a moment in silence.)

THE GIRL

Oh, I love that. I didn't even know it was from a show or anything. I thought it was just a song. . . .

RICHARD

Walter Huston sang it. He had a wooden leg—in the show. You better have some more champagne. It's really very good.

(He puts a little more in her glass which is still half full. He refills his own. She takes off her shoes.)

55

THE GIRL

This is pretty nice. . . .

RICHARD

Isn't it? It's a lot better than sitting out there listening to the ball game. Two runs behind and they send Hodges up to bunt!

THE GIRL

Is that bad?

RICHARD

It's awful.

THE GIRL

I didn't know. I was never very good at baseball. I was going to wash my hair tonight. But after I got through with the garden I just didn't feel like it.

RICHARD

I was going to bed and read *Of Sex and Violence* and *The Scarlet Letter*. We're publishing them in the fall and I'm supposed to read them.

THE GIRL

You're a book publisher?

RICHARD

In a way. I'm the advertising manager for a firm called Pocket Classics. Two bits in any drugstore. I'm supposed to figure out a new title for *The Scarlet Letter*. They want something a little catchier. . . .

THE GIRL

I think I read *The Scarlet Letter* in school. . . . I don't remember much about it. . . .

RICHARD

Neither do I. I sent a memo to Mr. Brady—he's the head of the company—advising him not to change the title. But we had the title tested and eighty per cent of the people didn't know what it meant. So we're changing it . . .

(*He gets up and fills glass again*)

Do you know what Mr. Brady wanted to call it?

(*She shakes her head*)

I Was an Adulteress. But he's not going to, thank God. And do you know why? Because we had *it* tested and sixty-three per cent of the people didn't know what *that* meant. I wish you'd drink some more of your champagne. . . .

THE GIRL

No, thanks . . .

(*She rises and drifts over to the bookcase*)

You've certainly got a lot of books. . . .

RICHARD

There're cases more in the closets. . . .

THE GIRL
(*Suddenly*)
Oh! Look! You've got *US Camera*!

RICHARD
(*A little flustered*)
Do we? I didn't even know it. How about that! *US Camera*!

THE GIRL
(*She takes it down*)
I bet I bought a dozen copies of this. But I don't have a single one left. Boys and people used to keep stealing 'em. . . .

RICHARD
I can't think why. . . .

THE GIRL
Did you ever notice me in it? It's a picture called "Textures."

RICHARD
I'm afraid I didn't. . . .

THE GIRL
I told you about it, don't you remember? See, that's me, right there on the beach. My hair was a little longer then, did you notice?

RICHARD
No, actually—I didn't . . .

58

THE GIRL

And of course I've taken off some weight. I weighed 124 then. Gene Belding—Gene took the picture—used to call it baby fat.

RICHARD

Baby fat?

THE GIRL

Mmm! I'm much thinner now. . . .
(*They both study the picture for a moment.*)

RICHARD

This was taken at the beach?

THE GIRL

Mmm . . .

RICHARD

What beach?

THE GIRL

Right on Fire Island . . . Oh . . . I see what you mean. It was taken very early in the morning. Nobody was even up yet.

RICHARD

Just you and Miss Belding?

THE GIRL

Mr. Belding. Gene Belding. With a G . . .

RICHARD

Oh. Well, it certainly is a fine picture.

THE GIRL

I'll autograph it for you if you want. People keep asking me to . . .

RICHARD
(*Weakly*)

That would be wonderful. . . . Maybe we'd better have some more champagne. . . .

THE GIRL

Good. You know, this is suddenly beginning to feel like a party. . . .

(*He refills her glass which is only half-empty and fills his own all the way, emptying the bottle*)

It was awfully sweet of you to ask me down here in the first place. . . .

(*He drains his glass of champagne—looks at her for a moment.*)

RICHARD

Oh, it was just one of those things. Just one of those foolish things. A trip to the moon—on gossamer wings . . . Do you play the piano?

THE GIRL

The piano?

RICHARD

Yeah. Somebody should play the piano. Do you play?

THE GIRL

I really don't. Do you?

RICHARD

Just a little. For myself . . .

THE GIRL

You play then . . .

RICHARD

You'll be sorry you asked. . . .

(*He sits at piano and after a very impressive moment begins to play "Chopsticks." She listens and is delighted.*)

THE GIRL

Oh! I was afraid you could *really* play. I can play *that* too!

(*She sits on the bench beside him and they play "Chopsticks" as a duet. When they finish:*)

RICHARD

That was lovely. . . .

(*His manner changes*)

Tell me, what would you say if, quite suddenly, I were to seize you in my . . . Hey, come here . . .

(*He reaches over and takes her in his arms.*)

THE GIRL

Hey, now wait a minute . . .

(*For a moment they bounce precariously around on the piano bench, then* RICHARD *loses his balance and they both fall off knocking over the bench with a crash and landing in a tangle of arms and legs.*)

RICHARD
(*Panic-stricken*)

Are you all right? I'm sorry—I don't know what happened —I must be out of my mind. . . .

THE GIRL

I'm fine . . .

RICHARD

I don't know what happened. . . .

THE GIRL

Well, I think I'd better go now. . . .

(*Putting on her shoes.*)

RICHARD

Please don't . . . I'm sorry . . .

THE GIRL

I'd better. Good night . . .

RICHARD

Please . . . I'm so sorry . . .

THE GIRL

That's all right. Good night.

(*She goes, closing the door behind her.*)

(RICHARD *looks miserably at the door. Then turns and kicks viciously at the piano bench. He succeeds in injuring his toe. Sadly, still shaking his wounded foot, he limps to the kitchen and reappears a moment later with a bottle of raspberry soda. He goes to the phonograph and puts on "September Song." He listens to it with morbid fascination. In a melancholy voice he joins Mr. Huston in a line or two about what a long, long while it is from May to December. He shakes his head and crosses sadly to the terrace. He stands there—a mournful figure clutching a bottle of raspberry soda.*)

(*As he stands there, a potted geranium comes crashing down from the terrace above and shatters at his feet.*)

(*He does not even bother to look around. He merely glances over his shoulder and says:*)

RICHARD

(*Quietly*)

Oh, now, for God's sake, let's not start that again. . . .

THE GIRL'S VOICE
(*From above*)

Oh, golly! I was just taking them in so there wouldn't be another accident. I'm really sorry. . . . I mean this is awful. . . . I could have practically killed you again. . . .

RICHARD

It doesn't matter. . . .

THE GIRL'S VOICE
(*From above*)

I'm really sorry. It was an accident. . . . Are you all right. . . ?

RICHARD

I'm fine.

THE GIRL'S VOICE
(*From above*)

Well, good night . . .

RICHARD

Good night . . .

THE GIRL'S VOICE
(*From above*)

Good night. See you tomorrow, maybe. . . .

RICHARD

Huh? (*He straightens up.*) Yeah! I'll see you tomorrow!

THE SEVEN YEAR ITCH

THE GIRL'S VOICE
(*From above*)

Good night!

(*He starts to drink from soda bottle. Stops himself. Puts it down in disgust. Then strides back to living room with renewed vigor. He goes to the liquor cabinet and begins to pour himself another drink. From the phonograph comes the happy chorus of "September Song."*)

(RICHARD, *a peculiar expression on his face, sings cheerfully with the record as:*)

The curtain falls

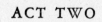

ACT TWO

ACT TWO

Scene I

The same.

It is early evening the following day. RICHARD, *back in full control and very businesslike, is deep in conference with* DR. BRUBAKER.

Both are somewhat tense and it is evident that the conference has been proceeding with difficulty. The DOCTOR *is seated amid a litter of papers and galley sheets.* RICHARD *holds a duplicate set of galleys. As the curtain rises* RICHARD *clears his throat and prepares to renew his attack.*

RICHARD

On page one hundred and ten, Doctor, if we could somehow simplify the whole passage . . .

DR. BRUBAKER

Simplify? In what way simplify?

RICHARD

In the sense of making it—well—simpler. Both Mr. Brady and I have gone over it a number of times, and, to be perfectly frank with you, neither of us has any clear idea of what it's actually about . . .

DR. BRUBAKER

Your Mr. Brady, sir, is, if I may also speak with frankness, a moron.

RICHARD

It is Mr. Brady's business, as an editor, to keep the point of view of the average reader very clearly in mind. If something is beyond Mr. Brady's comprehension, he can only assume that it will also be over the head of our readership.

DR. BRUBAKER

It was, I take it, at Mr. Brady's suggestion that the title of my book was changed from *Of Man and the Unconscious* to, and I shudder to say these words aloud, *Of Sex and Violence....*

RICHARD

That is correct. Mr. Brady felt that the new title would have a broader popular appeal.

DR. BRUBAKER

I regret to inform you, sir, that Mr. Brady is a psychopathic inferior....

RICHARD

Cheer up, Doctor. If you think you've got troubles, Mr. Brady wants to change *The Scarlet Letter* to *I Was an Adulteress.* I know it all seems a little odd to you—but Mr. Brady understands the twenty-five-cent book field. Both Mr. Brady and I *want* to publish worthwhile books. Books like yours. Like *The Scarlet Letter.* But you must remember that you and

Nathaniel Hawthorne are competing in every drugstore with
the basic writings of Mickey Spillane.

(*As* DR. BRUBAKER *is unacquainted with this author,*
RICHARD's *bon mot gets no reaction.*)

DR. BRUBAKER
This is therefore why my book is to be published with a
cover depicting Gustav Meyerheim in the very act of attack-
ing one of his victims. . . .

(DR. BRUBAKER *has picked up a large full-color paint-
ing of the cover of his book which shows in lurid
detail a wild-eyed man with a beard attempting to
disrobe an already pretty-well disrobed young lady.
It also bears the following line of copy: "Hotter Than
the Kinsey Report." Both regard the cover for a
moment.*)

RICHARD
(*With a certain nervous heartiness*)
I must take the responsibility for the cover myself,
Doctor. . . .

DR. BRUBAKER
And also for making Meyerheim's victim—all of whom in-
cidentally, were middle-aged women—resemble in a number
of basic characteristics, Miss Betty Grable?

RICHARD
I'm afraid so, Doctor. Don't you think there would be something just a little bit distasteful about a book jacket showing
a man attempting to attack a middle-aged lady?

DR. BRUBAKER

And it is less distasteful if the lady is young and beautiful?

RICHARD

At least, if a man attacks a young and beautiful girl, it seems more . . . Oh, my God!

(*He remembers last night and shudders.*)

DR. BRUBAKER

I beg your pardon?

RICHARD

Nothing. Doctor, if you don't like the cover, I'll see if I can have it changed. . . .

DR. BRUBAKER

I would be most grateful.

RICHARD

Doctor.

DR. BRUBAKER

Yes?

RICHARD

You say in the book that ninety per cent of the population is in need of some sort of psychiatric help?

DR. BRUBAKER

This is theoretically true. It is not however practical. There is the matter of cost. . . .

RICHARD

With your own patients—are you very expensive?

DR. BRUBAKER

(*His Third Ear has caught the direction this conversation is leading and his defenses go up immediately*)

Very.

RICHARD

I'm sure you occasionally make exceptions. . . .

DR. BRUBAKER

Never.

RICHARD

I mean, once in a while a case must come along that really interests you. . . .

DR. BRUBAKER

(*Primly*)

At fifty dollars an hour—all my cases interest me.

RICHARD

(*Undaunted*)

I mean if you should run into something really spectacular. Another Gustav Meyerheim, for example . . .

DR. BRUBAKER

If Meyerheim were alive today and desired my help it would cost him fifty dollars an hour, just like anyone else. . . .

73

RICHARD

Doctor, tell me frankly. Do you think, just for example, that *I* need to be psychoanalyzed?

DR. BRUBAKER

Very possibly. I could recommend several very excellent men who might, perhaps, be a little cheaper.

RICHARD

How much cheaper?

DR. BRUBAKER
(*Considering*)

Ohhhhh ...

RICHARD

I couldn't even afford *that*. ...

DR. BRUBAKER

I thought not. (*He turns back to his papers*) Now to get back to ...

RICHARD
(*Seating himself casually on the couch*)
I wondered if possibly you might give me some advice. ...

DR. BRUBAKER

I know. Everyone wonders that.

(*Still moving casually,* RICHARD *swings his feet onto the couch until he is lying in the classic position.*)

RICHARD

I'm desperate, Doctor. Last night after you left, I was just sitting there listening to the ball game ...

DR. BRUBAKER

(*Outmaneuvered, but still game*)

This fact in itself is not really sufficient cause to undertake analysis ...

RICHARD

No, I don't mean that. I *started out* listening to the ball game and do you know what I ended up doing?

DR. BRUBAKER

I have no idea. ...

RICHARD

I ended up attempting to commit what I guess they call criminal assault. ...

DR. BRUBAKER

(*Defeated, he takes a pad and pencil from his pocket*)

From the way you phrase it, I assume the attempt was unsuccessful. ...

RICHARD

Thank God! All I did was knock us both off the piano bench. ...

(*A flicker of interest—he begins to write*)

You attempted to commit criminal assault on a *piano bench?*

RICHARD

Yes.

DR. BRUBAKER

And on whose person was this obviously maladroit attempt committed?

(RICHARD *rises and goes to bookshelf. Gets* US Camera *and shows it to* DOCTOR.)

RICHARD

That's her. Her hair was a little longer then.

DR. BRUBAKER
(*After a moment*)

Splendid. I congratulate you on your taste. However, you ask for my advice. I give it to you. Do not attempt it again.

(*A brief pause while the* DOCTOR *re-examines the photograph*)

If you *should,* however, give yourself plenty of room to work in. In any case do not attempt it precariously balanced on a piano bench. Such an attempt is doomed from the start. Now, my boy, I must go. I have many things to . . .

RICHARD

But look, Doctor—I'm married. I've always been married. Suppose this girl tells people about this. She's likely to mention it to someone. Like my wife.

DR. BRUBAKER

This is, of course, not beyond the realm of possibility. In that event I would recommend a course of vigorous denial. It would be simply your word against hers. Very possibly, if you were convincing enough, you could make it stick. And now I must really go. I thank you for your help. It is agreed that I shall make the necessary clarifications in Chapter Eight and you will devote your best efforts to making the cover of my book look less like a French postal card. I shall be in touch with your office the first of next week. . . .

RICHARD

If she tells anyone about this—I'll, I'll—kill her! I'll kill her with my bare hands!

DR. BRUBAKER
(*Who has started to leave, turns back*)

This is also a possible solution. However, I submit that murder is the most difficult of all crimes to commit successfully. Therefore, until you are able to commit a simple criminal assault, I strongly advise that you avoid anything so complex as murder. One must learn to walk before one can run. I thank you again and good night.

(*He exits briskly.*)

(RICHARD *stands blankly staring after the good Doctor. He shakes his head.*)

(*Music sneaks in—he turns and there grouped about the couch and coffee table, in "dream lighting" are* HELEN, THE GIRL, MISS MORRIS, ELAINE, MARIE WHATEVER-HER-NAME-WAS *and an unidentified*

YOUNG LADY *in brassiere and panties. They all brandish tea cups and in very hen-party fashion are engaged in dishing the dirt about someone. It is, after all, a figment of* RICHARD's *imagination, so the cups are raised and lowered in unison and the little clucking noises of disapproval are done in chorus.*)

THE GIRL
(*Very chatty*)

Actually, Mrs. Sherman, it was terribly embarrassing. He seemed to go berserk. He'd been sitting playing "Chopsticks" when suddenly he grabbed me and practically tried to tear my clothes off. . . .

ELAINE

My dear, the night of your birthday party he made himself perfectly obnoxious right out there on the terrace. I don't like to say this, but he attempted to take advantage of me.

(*All the girls shake their heads and make small clucking noises of shocked disapproval.*)

MISS MORRIS

It's just terrible, Mrs. Sherman. I'm positively scared to go into his office to take dictation. Why, the way that man looks at me, it makes me feel kinda naked. . . .

(*All drink tea.*)

ELAINE

I said, Richard darling, at least have the decency not to try something like this practically in front of poor Helen's eyes!

THE GIRL

He'd been drinking heavily, of course. . . . He practically guzzled a whole bottle of my champagne. . . .

MARIE

(*In French*)

Madame! Madame! He was like a human beast! He tore off my belt, he tore off my shirt, he tore off my pants and he chased me into the sea without a bathing costume.

(*All shake heads and "Tsk-tsk." Then the unidentified* YOUNG LADY *in the bra and pants speaks up.*)

YOUNG LADY

And *me*! I'm not even safe in my own apartment! Every time I start getting ready for bed that man sits out there on the terrace—staring at me! I just hate a Peeping Tom!

HELEN

I've always suspected that Richard was not quite sane.

THE GIRL

Oh, he's sane, all right. He's just a nasty, evil-minded, middle-aged man. . . .

(RICHARD *can stand it no longer.*)

RICHARD

Helen! Listen to me. . . .

(*The girls raise their tea cups and vanish. Music in and out and lighting back to normal.*)

RICHARD

(*In a panic, lights a cigarette*)

I've got to do something. That girl's probably told fifty people about this already. If I just sent her some flowers . . . That's no good. . . . I've got to talk to her. Reason with her. Plead with her. Tell her I was drunk, which God knows I was, and beg her not to mention this to anyone or my life could be ruined. . . .

(*He has found telephone book and is riffling through pages*)

Twelve solid pages of Kaufman . . . Here it is . . . ORegon 3-7221.

(*He lifts receiver, starts to dial, then stops*)

I can't do it. What can I possibly say to her?

(*He practices—holding receiver switch down*)

RICHARD

(*With great charm*)

My dear Miss—*I don't even know what the hell her name is*—My dear Young Woman—I have simply called to apologize for my absurd behavior last night. It was inexcusable, but I had been drinking. I can barely remember what happened, but I'm under the impression that I made a terrible fool of myself. I beg you to forgive me and put the whole distasteful incident out of your mind.

(*Stops and puts down phone*)

No good. I can't do it.

And what about Helen? She hasn't called. She's probably heard about it by now. Oh, that's out of the question. How could she possibly have heard anything? But she could have. The word gets around. It's like jungle drums.

If she hasn't heard anything—why hasn't she called?

I could call her. The minute I heard her voice I could tell if she knew anything.

Come on. Call her.

Stop stalling. Pick up the telephone and call her. It's the only way you'll know.

Okay. Okay.

(*He picks up the phone and dials the Long-Distance Operator*)

Long Distance? I want to call Cohasset. Cohasset, Massachusetts 4-2831-J. Yeah . . . My number? ORegon 9-4437. Thank you.

Okay—fasten your seat belts. . . .

Hello? Hello, Helen? Who? Who is this? Look, I want to talk to Mrs. Richard Sherman. Is she there? Who is this anyway? Oh. The baby sitter. Look, this is Mr. Sherman calling from New York. What do you mean she's out for the evening. With whom is she out for the evening? Mr. MacKenzie and some people? *What people?* Well, what *was* the message she left for me?

Oh. Oh, my God. Her yellow skirt. No, no, I didn't. Something unexpected came up. But tell her I will. The first thing in the morning. Without fail.

Look, I want to ask you. How did Mrs. Sherman seem? I mean did she seem upset in anyway? Like she'd heard some bad news or anything like that?

81

Just about the yellow skirt. Well, good. Tell her I'll send it up the first thing in the morning. Is Ricky all right? Good. When Mrs. Sherman comes in, tell her everything is fine here and I'll talk to her tomorrow. . . . Fine . . . Good-bye . . . Good-bye.

(He hangs up phone)

Well, thank God!

(He sits down and lights a cigarette)

The only thing I cannot understand is, what the hell is she doing having dinner with Tom MacKenzie. I wish she wouldn't hang around with people like that. He gets away with murder because he's a writer. Well, he's a damn lousy writer. That last book!

Helen should know better than to go around with people like that. She isn't even safe.

I know for a positive fact that he's been after her for years. Tom MacKenzie happens to be a real bum, if you want to know! And there probably aren't any other people.

She doesn't know what she's getting herself into. She's been married so long she forgets what it's like.

Helen happens to be a damned attractive woman. A man like Tom MacKenzie is perfectly capable of making a pass at her.

(By now he has begun to pace the floor)

And don't think she doesn't know what she's doing. She's getting older. She's used to me. In many ways I'm probably very dull. And Tom MacKenzie's a writer. She probably thinks he's fascinating as hell!

She thought that last book of his was great! All that inwardly-downwardly-pulsating-and-afterward-her-hair-spilled-across-the-pillow crap! Strictly for little old ladies at Womrath's.

But Helen is just the kind of middle-aged dame who would fall for it.

Well, good luck! That's all!

(*Brooding, he sits in easy chair, a grim expression on his face.*)

(*Music sneaks in and the "dream lighting" comes up on the far side of the stage by the fireplace. We hear the sound of wind mingled with the music. A door opens and slams shut and* TOM MACKENZIE *and* HELEN *enter, laughing.* TOM MACKENZIE *is a handsome, glamorous-type author with a mustache. He looks quite a lot like his photograph on the book jackets. He wears a tweed coat with the collar up and a hunting shirt.* HELEN *wears a sweater and skirt with a man's raincoat thrown about her shoulders. Both are very gay.*)

HELEN
(*As he helps her off with raincoat*)

It's been years since I took a walk on the beach in the rain. . . .

TOM
I love the rain on the sea. It's so wild and untamed. . . .

HELEN
(*Looking around*)
Where are the other people?

TOM
I have a confession to make.

HELEN
Yes?

TOM
There are no other people. Don't be angry.

HELEN
(*After a moment*)
I'm not angry.

TOM
I hoped you wouldn't be. Come over here by the fire.

HELEN
I love an open fire.

TOM
I always say, What good is the rain without an open fire?

RICHARD
(*From his chair across the room*)
Oh, brother!

TOM

Let me get you a little whiskey to take out the chill. . . .

HELEN

Thank you . . .

> (*He pours whiskey from flask. She drinks, then hands the cup to him. He drinks—but first kisses the spot on the cup where her lips have been.*)

RICHARD
> (*Muttering scornfully*)

H.B. Warner . . .

TOM

But wait. You're shivering. . . .

HELEN

It's nothing. I'll be warm in a moment. . . .

TOM

No, no . . . You're soaked to the skin. You'll catch your death of cold. . . .

RICHARD

Here it comes. . . .

TOM

Why don't you take off your things and hang them by the fire? I'll get you something dry. . . .

RICHARD
(*Appalled*)
He used *that* in his book, for God's sake! As who didn't!

HELEN
All right. Turn your back...

> (*He turns his back and she removes her shoes. She takes off her skirt and hangs it on the fire screen.*)

TOM
May I turn around now?

HELEN
If you like...

> (*Suddenly, the mood has changed. His voice is now husky with passion.*)

TOM
Helen, darling!

HELEN
Yes, Tom?

TOM
Did anyone ever tell you that you are a very beautiful woman?

HELEN
No. Not recently anyway...

TOM

But surely Richard . . .

HELEN

I'm afraid Richard rather takes me for granted now. . . .

TOM

That blind, utter fool!

HELEN

Oh, darling!

TOM

Darling!

(*The music swells.* TOM *takes her in his arms.*)
(*Murmuring as he covers her with kisses*)

Inwardly, downwardly, pulsating, striving, now together, ending and unending, now, now, now!

(*They are in a full mad clinch as the lights black out.*)

(*On his side of the room,* RICHARD *jumps to his feet and angrily pounds the table.*)

RICHARD

Okay! If that's the way you want it! Okay!

(*With great purpose he strides to the telephone. Gets phone book, thumbs through it, finds number and dials. He whistles softly through his teeth. . . . The tune he is whistling might, if he were not tone deaf, almost be "Just One of Those Things." After a moment someone obviously answers the phone.*)

RICHARD
(*With great charm*)
Hi. Did you know you left your tomato plant down here last night? I could have the janitor bring it back—or—if you want—I was thinking maybe I could . . .

(*He is talking into the phone with great animation by the time the lights have dimmed and:*)

The curtain is down

ACT TWO

SCENE II

The same. It is later that evening.

The apartment is empty. A single light in the foyer.

After a moment, the sound of a key in the lock and RICH-
ARD *and the* GIRL *enter. He switches on the lights.*

RICHARD

Well, we made it.

THE GIRL

I'm so full of steak I can barely wobble....

RICHARD

Me too.

THE GIRL

I feel wonderful....

RICHARD

Did anyone ever tell you that you have a very, very beautiful digestive tract?

THE GIRL

Yes. But they don't usually say it like that. Mostly they
just say: Boy, did you ever stuff yourself!

RICHARD

Would you like a drink or something?

THE GIRL

No, thanks. But you go ahead and have one. Don't mind me . . .

RICHARD

Not me. I'm back on the wagon again. . . .

THE GIRL

This was awfully nice of you. It was enough to have you carry that heavy plant all the way upstairs. You didn't have to ask me out for dinner. I hope you didn't hurt yourself. Or strain something . . .

RICHARD

It wasn't that heavy. I was going to call the janitor to help me, but then I decided not to. . . .

THE GIRL

You're in pretty good shape. . . .

RICHARD

For an old man . . .

THE GIRL

You're not *that* old. You don't look a day over twenty-eight.

RICHARD

I know. . . .

THE GIRL

Anyway it was very nice of you.

RICHARD

I just took a chance and called. I didn't really think you'd be home. You know, I thought you'd be out or something.

THE GIRL

No, I don't go out very much. . . .

RICHARD

That's funny. I should think you'd have a line of suitors halfway round the block. Like Easter show at Radio City . . .

THE GIRL

Last night, I went to the movies by myself. . . .

RICHARD

Last night?

THE GIRL
(*Diplomatically*)

After I left here.

RICHARD
(*Moving the conversation past a trouble spot*)

All by yourself! You must have a boy friend or something. . . .

THE GIRL

I don't go out with most people who ask me. I know it sounds silly but people are always falling desperately in love with me and everything and it makes things so complicated. I mean, it's just easier to pay the fifty-five cents and go to the movies by yourself.

RICHARD

It doesn't sound very exciting. . . .

THE GIRL

It is, though. This is the first time I've had my own apartment and everything.

RICHARD

You went out with me when I asked you. . . .

THE GIRL

Well, that's different. I mean, it's all right going out with you. After all, you're married.

RICHARD

I see. I *think*.

THE GIRL

No. What I mean is, it's all right to have dinner with you because you're not likely to fall desperately in love with me or anything. You're more mature. . . .

RICHARD

I don't feel so—mature. . . .

THE GIRL

Well, you know what I mean.

(*Pause.*)

RICHARD

You're absolutely sure you wouldn't like a drink?

THE GIRL

Absolutely.

RICHARD

I think maybe I'll have one. Just a little one.

(*He goes to bar and fixes himself a drink*)

Not even a Coke or something?

THE GIRL

Not right now.

RICHARD

Well, happy birthday.
  (*Pause.*)

THE GIRL

This certainly is a beautiful apartment.

RICHARD

It's all right. It's a little ridiculous in some ways. . . . The stairs, for instance . . .

THE GIRL

I think they're beautiful. I like an apartment with stairs.

RICHARD

But these don't go any place. They just go up to the ceiling and stop. They give the joint a kind of Jean Paul Sartre quality.

THE GIRL

I see what you mean. No exit. A stairway to nowhere.

RICHARD

I tried to get the landlord to take them out. See, this used to be the bottom half of a duplex. This place and the Kaufmans' were all one apartment. So when he divided them separately he just boarded up the ceiling—or in your case the floor ...

THE GIRL

Yes, I noticed the place in the floor. I lost an orange stick down the crack. Anyway, I think the apartment's just charming....

RICHARD

Yeah. But we're moving into a larger place in September....

THE GIRL

Oh, that's too bad. But still, people in New York are always moving. You certainly have a lot of books. The last book I read was *The Catcher in the Rye* ...

RICHARD

The last book I read was *The Scarlet Letter*. Mr. Brady thinks we can sell it. If we make it sound sexy enough.

THE GIRL

Is it sexy? I don't seem to remember.

RICHARD

No. Actually, it's kind of dull. In fact, people are going to want their quarters back. But Mr. Brady feels we can sell it if I can just figure out a way to tell people what the Scarlet Letter is.

THE GIRL
What *is* it?

RICHARD
Well, The Scarlet Letter was a big red "A". For Adultery. Anyone who was convicted of adultery had to wear it.

THE GIRL
How awful!

RICHARD
The cover will be a picture of Hester Prynne with a cigarette hanging out of her mouth. She'll be in a real tight, low-cut dress. Our big problem is—if the dress is cut low enough to sell any copies, there won't be any space on the front for a big red letter . . .

THE GIRL
The publishing business sounds fascinating.

RICHARD
Oh, it is. It is.

(*Pause.*)

THE GIRL
It's getting late. I really ought to go. . . .

RICHARD
You've got plenty of time.

95

THE GIRL

I guess so. That's the wonderful thing about having my own apartment. I mean at the club you had to be in at one o'clock or they locked the doors.

RICHARD

It sounds barbaric. . . .

THE GIRL

Oh, it practically was. It was really very funny. I mean, all the girls at the club were actresses. So naturally they were always asking each other what they called the big question. . . .

RICHARD

The big question?

THE GIRL

Mmm! They were always asking each other: Would you sleep with a producer to get a part?

RICHARD

That is a big question. . . .

THE GIRL

But it's so silly. If you live at the club anyway. I used to tell them, producers don't even *go* to bed before one o'clock. So the whole thing is academic, if you see what I mean. You'd be surprised how much time they spent discussing it, though.

RICHARD

I can see where they might give the matter some thought.

THE GIRL

Oh, sure. But they never discussed it in a *practical* way. When they asked me, I always used to say: It depends. How big is the part? Is the producer handsome? Things like that ...

RICHARD

Practical things ...

THE GIRL

Mmm! I was at the club for eight months and as far as I know no producer ever mentioned the subject to any of the girls.

RICHARD

That must have been very disappointing for them.

THE GIRL

It was.

RICHARD

But what if he was very handsome? And it was a very good part? And you didn't have to be in by one o'clock? What *would* you do?

THE GIRL

In that case ... If I was sure he wouldn't fall desperately in love with me and ask me to marry him and everything.

RICHARD

What's so bad about that?

THE GIRL

Oh, that would spoil everything. Marrying him, I mean. It would be worse than living at the club. Then I'd have to start getting in at one o'clock again. I mean it's taken me twenty-two years to get my own apartment. It would be pretty silly if the first thing I did was get married and spoil everything. I mean, I want to have a chance to be independent first. For a few years anyway. You can't imagine how exciting it is to live by yourself—after you've had somebody practically running your life for as long as you can remember. . . . You just can't imagine . . .

(*As* RICHARD *stops listening to the* GIRL *and gradually becomes absorbed in his own thoughts, the lights dim down till there is only a dream spot on* RICHARD.)

RICHARD

Yes, I can. As a matter of fact we have a great deal in common.

HIS VOICE

(*Mockingly—imitating* HELEN's *tone*)

Daddy's going to work very hard. And he's going to stay on the wagon, like Dr. Summers told him. And he's going to eat properly and not smoke, like Dr. Murphy told him. And Mommy is going to call Daddy tonight just to make sure he's all right . . .

Poor Daddy!

RICHARD

Poor Daddy!

THE SEVEN YEAR ITCH

HIS VOICE

The girl is absolutely right. Not want to get married. You
—you dope. The minute you were old enough to have any
fun—the only thing you could think of to do was to get
married.

RICHARD

I know. I know. It was a kind of nervousness. But I made
the best of it. I've been a pretty good husband. When I think
of the chances I've had . . .

HIS VOICE

We've been through all this before. . . .

RICHARD

I know. I know. I just thought I'd mention it.

HIS VOICE

Has it ever dawned on you that you're kidding yourself?

RICHARD

What do you mean by that?

HIS VOICE

All those dames you could have had if you weren't such
a noble husband. The only reason you didn't do anything
about 'em is that you didn't want to. . . .

RICHARD

Why didn't I want to?

99

HIS VOICE

Laziness, pal. Laziness. It was too much trouble. You just
didn't want to get involved. Elaine, for instance. It would
have taken six months. And all those phone calls and taxis
and excuses.

RICHARD

Yeah. (*Pause*) Why does it always have to be so
complicated?

HIS VOICE

If you could answer that one, pal-pal, they'd make you
President of the United States.

(RICHARD *sighs and the lights dim back to normal.
The* GIRL *is still speaking, unaware of the fact that
his mind has been far away.*)

THE GIRL

. . . . so when you asked me to go out for dinner with you
it was all right. You're married and naturally, you don't want
to fall desperately in love with anyone any more than I want
anyone to fall desperately in love with me. Do you know what
I mean?

RICHARD

Sure. It's too much trouble.

THE GIRL

Exactly.

RICHARD

I know just what you mean.

100

THE GIRL

That's right.

RICHARD

We both happen to be in positions where we can't possibly let ourselves get involved in anything. . . .

THE GIRL

Mmm.

RICHARD

All the damn phone calls and taxis and everything.

THE GIRL

That's right. I mean I certainly wouldn't be sitting alone with some man in his apartment at eleven-thirty at night if he wasn't married.

RICHARD

Certainly not. (*Pause*) When you said about the producer —it would depend on if he were handsome—what did you mean by that? I mean, just out of curiosity. . . . what would be your idea of handsome?

THE GIRL

Well, let's see. I really don't know. I suppose he should be tall—and kind of mature-looking . . .

RICHARD

Like me?

101

THE GIRL
(*Thoughtfully*)

Mmmmm . . . (*Pause*) You're not going to start falling desperately in love with me or anything, are you?

RICHARD

No. No. Definitely not. I mean I think you're very pretty and sweet and I certainly enjoyed having dinner with you. But . . .

THE GIRL

That's just the way *I* feel about you. You're very nice-looking and charming and mature. You're someone I can be with and count on him not falling desperately in love with me. . . .

RICHARD

That's right. I'm almost—well—I'm a lot older than you are. And one thing I've learned. Nothing is ever as simple as you think it's going to be. You take the simplest damn thing and, before you know it, it gets all loused up. I don't know how it happens or why it happens but it always happens. . . .

THE GIRL

That's very true. You're absolutely right.

(*As the* GIRL *stops listening to* RICHARD *and gradually becomes absorbed in her own thoughts the lights dim to a single dream spot on her.*)

HER VOICE

Well, what do you think?

THE GIRL

Mmm . . .

HER VOICE

What do you mean—mmm?

THE GIRL

I mean—I don't know . . .

HER VOICE

That's ridiculous. What is there not to know? He certainly is nice—and he's mature without being—you know—decrepit or anything . . .

THE GIRL

He certainly seems well-preserved. . . .

HER VOICE

He's sweet and intelligent and married. What more do you want?

THE GIRL

I don't know.

HER VOICE

You're the one who wants to be the big-deal woman of the world. It's all your idea. It's not as if you were some kind of a virginal creature or something.

103

THE GIRL

Oh—shut up—I mean you make it sound so—so clinical. Besides, you certainly can't count Jerry . . .

HER VOICE

What do you mean we can't count Jerry?

THE GIRL

Well, I mean it was a big mistake—and it was so—so—and then he got all hysterical and wanted to marry me. . . .

HER VOICE

It counts.

THE GIRL

I mean you can understand a person wanting to find out something about life and everything before she gets married and all settled down and has to start getting in by one o'clock again. . . . Besides, what makes you think he's interested in me that way? I must seem like some kind of a juvenile delinquent to him. . . .

HER VOICE

You're twenty-two years old. And he's interested.

THE GIRL

How can you tell?

HER VOICE

I can tell. . . .

THE GIRL

How?

HER VOICE

I can tell. . . . What have you got to lose?

THE GIRL

Well, nothing, I guess—if you're really going to make Jerry count.

HER VOICE

He counts . . .

THE GIRL

Well, then . . .

(*The lights come back to normal.* RICHARD *is still talking, unaware that the* GIRL'S *mind has been far away.*)

RICHARD

. . . what I'm trying to say is, that people who are really mature weigh things more carefully. They impose a discipline on themselves. They understand the cost. . . . I mean, they finally learn that sometimes something that seems very wonderful and desirable isn't really worth . . . I mean—all the hysteria it's going to cause . . . (*Pause*) Then, of course, you can overdo that line of thinking too. I mean a man—a person—anyone doesn't like to feel he's some kind of a vegetable or something. You know. What it amounts to is this: You've got to decide which is the most painful—doing something and regretting it—or not doing something and—regretting it. Do you see what I mean?

THE GIRL

I think so. . . .

RICHARD

I didn't mean to start making a speech. Look, are you sure you don't want a drink?

THE GIRL

No, thanks. Really.

(*Starts to go.*)

RICHARD

Now look, really. It's not late. You don't have to go yet....

THE GIRL

I really should ...

RICHARD

Well, whatever you think. Let me take you up to your door....

THE GIRL

No. That's all right. It's just upstairs....

RICHARD

Well, all right. If you have to go.

THE GIRL

I want to thank you for the dinner. It was lovely....

RICHARD

It was fun....

THE GIRL

And for carrying that heavy plant all the way upstairs ...

RICHARD

It wasn't so heavy. . . .

(*They have edged almost to the door by now.*)

THE GIRL

Well, good night. And thanks—again . . .

RICHARD

Well, good night . . . (*She leans forward and kisses him lightly on the cheek*) Well, good night . . .

(*Suddenly they move together in a tight embrace which they hold for a moment. She breaks away, then kisses him again and in the same motion goes quickly out the door closing it behind her.*)

(RICHARD *is visibly shaken. He starts after her. Stops himself. Closes the door again. And locks it. He shakes his head and then puts on the chain lock.*)

(*Comes inside, starts for the phone, stops again. Tries to pull himself together. Picks up the galley sheets and sits down on the couch and tries to work on them.*)

(*As he sits, a square in the ceiling at the top of the stairs lifts out and a moment later the girl appears. She backs down the first few steps, lowering the floor-ceiling back into place. He is oblivious to this. She turns and starts down the stairs. We see that she is carrying a small claw hammer.*)

(*Quietly she comes down into the room. She looks at him and smiles. She pauses for a moment.*)

THE GIRL
(*With a small, ineffectual wave of the hand*)

Hi...

(RICHARD *almost jumps out of his skin. He sees her. After a moment he sees the hammer and realizes where she has come from. Then, after a long time, he smiles and makes a similar, ineffectual wave of the hand*)

RICHARD

Hi...

Curtain

ACT THREE

ACT THREE

The same.

It is about eight o'clock the following morning. The blinds on the French doors are drawn, but outside the sun is shining brightly. It is going to be another hot day.

As the curtain rises, RICHARD *stands by the French doors. He is in his shirt sleeves. He opens the blinds and then the doors. He steps out onto the terrace and breathes deeply. He comes back into the living room and notices the girl's shoes. Somewhat tentatively, he picks them up and carries them to the bedroom doors. He stops and listens a moment. He puts the shoes back where he found them and goes to the front door. He listens again, then unlocks the door without unfastening the chain.*

He kneels down and reaching around through the slightly open door fishes in milk and the newspaper. He carries the paper down to the armchair and tries to read. He can't, however.

After a moment he looks up and speaks to himself in a very reassuring voice.

RICHARD

There's not a thing in the world to worry about. Two very attractive, intelligent people happened to meet under circumstances that seemed to be—propitious—and, well, it happened. It was very charming and gay. As a matter of fact it was wonderful. But now it's over.

(He rises and starts for the bedroom)

We'll say good-bye, like two intelligent people. We'll have coffee ...

(He knocks gently on the door. He listens. He knocks again. His calm is rapidly evaporating)

How can she possibly sleep like that?

What's the matter with her anyway? Maybe she's sick or something. Maybe she's dead.

Maybe the excitement was too much for her and she passed away in her sleep.

Oh, my God! That means the police. And the reporters. "Actress found dead in publisher's apartment"!

(He looks desperately around. His eye lights on the staircase)

No. No. I'll just haul the body upstairs. That's all. Right back upstairs, nail up the floor again and that's all. They'd have no reason to suspect me. I'd wear gloves, of course. They'd never prove a thing.

Now stop it. You're getting hysterical again.

(Pause)

Well, if she isn't dead, why the hell doesn't she just get up and go home? It's late! It's—late—it's *really* late—it's ...

(He picks up his wrist watch from table)

... *ten after eight*? It seemed later than *that*. ...

(He is somewhat relieved by the time)

Well. I'll give her another half hour to catch up on her beauty sleep. Then, I'll very politely wake her. We'll have coffee like two intelligent people. And then, I'll kiss her good-bye.

> (*Confidently acting out the scene*)

It's been fun, darling, but now, of course, it's over . . . No tears—no regrets . . .

> (*He stands waving as if she were walking up the stairs*)

Just good-bye. It's been—swell . . .

> (*He blows a kiss upward, waves and then stands transfixed, a foolish expression on his face.*)

HIS VOICE

Pal.

RICHARD

Huh?

HIS VOICE

I don't want you to get upset or anything, but it might not be as easy as all that. You know. Be realistic.

RICHARD

What? What are you talking about?

HIS VOICE

I was just pointing out. Women don't take these things as lightly as men, you know. There *could* be complications. For example, suppose she's fallen desperately in love with you. . . .

RICHARD

She can't do that. It isn't fair. She knows she can't.

HIS VOICE

After all, pal, you had a little something to do with this yourself. . . .

RICHARD

Don't worry. I can handle it. Just don't worry. I can be tough if I have to. I can be pretty damn tough. If I set my mind to it, I can be a terrible heel. . . .

HIS VOICE
(*Mocking*)

Ha-*ha*!

RICHARD

Shut up . . .

(*He stands for a moment, setting his mind to being a terrible heel. The lights dim and music sneaks in. "Dream lighting" lights up the bedroom doors. They open and the girl emerges. She is dressed like an Al Parker illustration for a story called "Glorious Honeymoon" in* The Woman's Home Companion. *She is radiant.*)

THE GIRL
(*Radiantly*)

Good morning, my darling . . . Good morning . . . Good morning . . .

RICHARD

(*Very tough. He lights a cigarette and stares at her for a moment through ice-blue eyes*)

Oh. It's about time you dragged your dead pratt out of the sack. . . .

THE GIRL

Oh, darling, darling, darling . . . (*He exhales smoke*) What is it, my darling, you seem troubled . . .

RICHARD

Shut up, baby, and listen to me. I got something to tell you.

THE GIRL

And I've something to tell you. I've grown older, somehow, overnight. I know now that all our brave talk of independence—our not wanting to get involved—our being—actually —*afraid* of love—it was all childish nonsense. I'm not afraid to say it, darling. I love you. I want you. You belong to me.

RICHARD

Look, baby. Let's get one thing straight. I belong to nobody, see. If some dumb little dame wants to throw herself at me—that's her lookout, see. I'm strictly a one-night guy. I've left a string of broken hearts from here to—to Westport, Connecticut, and back. Now, the smartest little move you could make is to pack your stuff and scram. . . .

THE GIRL

Go? Not I! Not now! Not ever! Don't you see, my darling, after what we've been to each other . . .

RICHARD

I spell trouble, baby, with a capital "T". We're poison to each other—you and me. Don't you see that?

THE GIRL

When two people care for each other as we do . . .

RICHARD
(A little "PAL JOEY" creeping in)

What do I care for a dame? Every damn dame is the same. I'm going to own a night club. . . .

THE GIRL

That doesn't matter. Nothing matters. This thing is bigger than both of us. We'll *flaunt* our love. Shout it from the highest housetops. We're on a great toboggan. We can't stop it. We can't steer it. It's too late to run, the Beguine has begun . . .

RICHARD
(Weakly)

Oh, Jesus Christ . . .

THE GIRL
(Coolly taking charge)

Now then. Do you want to be the one to tell Helen, or shall I?

RICHARD
(With an anguished moan)

Tell Helen?

THE GIRL

Of course. We must. It's the only way. . . .

RICHARD

No, no, no! You can't do that! You can't!

(*He is now kneeling at her feet, pleading. She puts her arm about his shoulder. From somewhere comes the brave sound of a solo violin which plays behind her next speech.*)

THE GIRL

We can and we must. We'll face her together. Hand in hand. Proudly. Our heads held high. Oh, we'll be social outcasts, but we won't care. It'll be you and I together against the world. I'll go and dress now, darling. But I wanted you to know how I felt. I couldn't wait to tell you. Good-bye, for now, my darling. I won't be long . . .

(*As the music swells, she floats off into the bedroom, waving and blowing kisses with both hands. The "dream light" fades out and the lighting returns to normal.* RICHARD *stands panic-stricken in the middle of the living-room floor. He shakes his head.*)

RICHARD

I'm crazy. I'm going crazy. That's all. I've run amok. Helen goes away and I run amok. Raping and looting and . . . (*He notices the cigarette in his hand*) smoking cigarettes . . .

(*He quickly puts out the cigarette*)

117

What have I done? What did I think I was doing? What did I possibly think I was doing?

Damn it! I begged Helen not to go away for the summer. I begged her!

What am I going to do! That girl in there undoubtedly expects me to get a divorce and marry her.

HIS VOICE

Well, why don't you?

RICHARD

Are you kidding? What about Helen?

HIS VOICE

What about her? Maybe this is all for the best. Maybe this is the best thing that could have happened to you. After all, Helen's not as young as she used to be. In a couple of years you'll look like her son.

RICHARD

Now wait a minute. Wait a minute. Helen is still pretty attractive. She happens to be a damn beautiful woman, if you want to know. And we've been through a lot together. The time I was fired from Random House. And when little Ricky was sick—and I caught the damn mumps from him. She's taken a lot of punishment from me, if you want to know. And she's been pretty nice about it . . .

118

HIS VOICE

The point, however is: Do you love her?

RICHARD

Love her? Well, sure. Sure, I love her. Of course I love her. I'm *used to her*!

HIS VOICE

Used to her? That doesn't sound very exciting. Of course I imagine when a man enters middle life, he doesn't want someone exciting. He wants someone comfortable. Someone he's *used to* ...

RICHARD

Now, just a second. You've got the wrong idea. Helen's not so—*comfortable*. She's pretty exciting. You should see the way people look at her at parties and on the street and everywhere....

HIS VOICE

What people?

RICHARD

Men. That's what people. For instance, Tom MacKenzie, if you want to know. When Helen wears that green dress— the backless one with hardly any front—there's nothing comfortable about that at all ...

(RICHARD *sinks into chair and leans back*)

She wore it one night last spring when Tom MacKenzie was over—and you just couldn't get him out of here....

(*Music sneaks in and the lights dim. "Dream light-ing" fills the stage*)

It looked like he was going to go home about four different times but he just couldn't tear himself away . . .

(TOM *and* HELEN *appear.* HELEN *is wearing the green dress. It is everything* RICHARD *has said it is.*)

TOM

Helen, you look particularly lovely tonight. . . .

HELEN

Why, thank you, Tom . . .

TOM

You're a lucky boy, Dickie, even if you don't know it.

RICHARD

I know all about it and don't call me Dickie. . . .

TOM

Helen—Helen, that name is so like you. "Helen, thy beauty is to me as those Nicaean barks of yore" . . .

HELEN

Gracious . . .

TOM

No, no, I mean it. Stand there a moment. Let me drink you
in. Turn around. Slowly, that's it . . . (HELEN *models dress*)
You look particularly lovely in a backless gown . . .

RICHARD
(*Muttering*)

Backless, frontless, topless, bottomless, I'm on to you, you
son of a bitch . . .

TOM
(*From across the room*)

What was that, old man?

HELEN
(*Quickly*)

Don't pay any attention to Dick. You know what happens
to him and martinis. . . .

RICHARD

Two martinis. Two lousy martinis.

HELEN

Dr. Summers has told him time and time again that he
should go on the wagon for a while till his stomach gets
better. . . .

TOM

That's good advice, Dick. When a man can't handle the
stuff he should leave it alone completely. That's what I say.
Once a year—just to test my will power—I stop everything.

RICHARD
(*He starts to say something, but finally stops himself*)
No comment.

HELEN
(*Leaping once again into the breach*)
You really like this dress—do you, Tom?

TOM
I certainly do. It's a Potter original, isn't it?

HELEN
Yes—but that's wonderful! How did you know?

TOM
I'm a bit of an authority on women's clothes. You should really take me with you the next time you go shopping. We could have a bite of lunch first and really make a day of it. . . .

(*He has finally got to the door*)

Good night, Dick . . .

(RICHARD *waves unenthusiastically*)

Good night, Helen . . .

(*He kisses her.*)

HELEN
Good night, Tom . . .

TOM
I'll call you one day next week. . . .

HELEN

I'll be looking forward to it. (*She closes the door behind him*) I thought he was never going home . . .

RICHARD

(*In rather feeble imitation of* TOM)

"Helen, thy beauty is to me as those Nicaean barks of yore"—is he kidding?

HELEN

You know Tom. He beats his chest and makes noises but it doesn't really mean anything. . . .

RICHARD

I know. His Nicaean bark is worse than his Nicaean bite. . . . (*He is pleasantly surprised by how well this came out*) Hey, that's pretty good. That came out better than I thought it was going to. Nicaean bark—Nicaean bite . . .

HELEN

(*Unfractured*)

Actually, in some ways, Tom is very sweet. I mean it's nice to have people notice your clothes. . . .

RICHARD

Notice your clothes! He did a lot more than notice. . . . He practically . . . You know, you really ought to do something about that dress. Just the front part there . . .

HELEN

Do something about it?

RICHARD

I mean sort of . . . (*He gestures ineffectually about raising or tightening or something the front*) I don't know. Maybe we ought to empty the ash trays or something. You should see the way he was looking at you . . .

HELEN

You should have been flattered. Don't you want people to think your wife is attractive?

RICHARD

Sure, but . . . Why don't we clean this place up a little? It looks like a cocktail lounge on West Tenth Street. . . .

> (*He picks up an ash tray full of cigarette butts.*)
> (HELEN *comes over to him.*)

HELEN

Darling . . .

RICHARD

We ought to at least empty the ash trays . . .

HELEN

Not now . . .

RICHARD

(*Looks at her questioningly*)
Huh?

HELEN
I mean not now ...

> (*He looks at her for another moment and then very casually tosses away the tray full of butts and takes her in his arms.*)
> (*The lights black out and the music swells in the darkness.*)
> (*When the lights come on again the lighting is back to normal and* RICHARD *is leaning back in the chair where we left him, a self-satisfied grin on his face*)

HIS VOICE
Then you really do love Helen?

RICHARD
What do you want—an affidavit?

HIS VOICE
Well, good. So that leaves you with only one problem. I'm warning you, pal, it may not be as easy to get rid of this girl as you think.

RICHARD
Huh?

HIS VOICE
My dear boy, did you ever hear of a thing called blackmail?

RICHARD
Blackmail?

HIS VOICE

One often hears of unscrupulous young girls who prey on foolish, wealthy, middle-aged men. ...

RICHARD

Now, really ...

HIS VOICE

You got her into bed without any great effort. Why do you suppose she was so willing?

RICHARD

(*Weakly*)

But she said—she told me—she went on record—she didn't want to get involved ... (HIS VOICE *laughs coarsely*) A minute ago you were saying she was madly in love with me. ...

HIS VOICE

You poor, foolish, wealthy, middle-aged man.

RICHARD

Wait a minute—in the first place I'm not wealthy. ...

HIS VOICE

Blackmail, pal, it happens every day. She'll bleed you white.

RICHARD

Oh, my God. I'll have to sell the kid's bonds. . . . Poor Ricky. Poor Helen. There's only one thing to do. Confess everything and throw myself on her mercy. We're both intelligent people. She'll forgive me.

HIS VOICE

I wouldn't be a bit surprised if she shot you dead.

RICHARD

You're out of your mind. Not Helen. If she shot anyone it would much more likely be herself. Oh, my God. She'd probably shoot us both . . . I can't go on torturing myself like this. I'll have to tell her. Oh, she'll be hurt. For a while. But she'll get over it. There's no other way. I've got to tell her and take my chances. . . .

(*Music and "dream lighting" in.*)

RICHARD
(*Calling*)

Helen! Helen!

HELEN
(*From kitchen*)

Yes, darling . . .

RICHARD

Can you come in here a moment, please? There's something I must tell you.

(HELEN *enters from the kitchen. This is the domestic,
very un-green-dress* HELEN. *She wears an apron and
carries a bowl which she stirs with a wooden spoon*)

HELEN
(Sweetly)
Yes, Dick? I was just making a cherry pie. I know how
you hate the pies from Gristede's and I wanted to surprise
you. . . .

RICHARD
I don't know how to say this to you. . . .

HELEN
Yes, Dick?

RICHARD
We've been married a long time. . . .

HELEN
Seven years, darling. Seven glorious years. These are sweet-
heart cherries . . .

RICHARD
And in all that time, I've never looked at another
woman. . . .

HELEN
I know that, Dick. And I want to tell you what it's meant
to me. You may not know this, darling, but you're terribly
attractive to women. . . .

RICHARD

I am?

HELEN

Yes, you funny Richard you—you are. But in all those seven years I've never once worried. Oh, don't I know there are plenty of women who would give their eye teeth to get you. Elaine. Miss Morris. That Marie Whatever-her-name-was up in Westport. But I trust you, Dick. I always have. I always will. Do you know something?

RICHARD

What?

HELEN

I . . . Oh, I can't even say it. It's too foolish. . . .

RICHARD

Go ahead. Go ahead, say it. Be foolish.

HELEN

Well—I honestly believe that if you were ever unfaithful to me—I'd know it. I'd know it instantly.

RICHARD

You would?

HELEN

Oh, yes . . .

RICHARD

How?

HELEN

Wives have ways. Little ways.

RICHARD

And what would you do?

HELEN

Oh, darling, don't be ...

RICHARD

No. Really. I'm interested. What would you do?

HELEN

Oh, I think I'd probably shoot you dead. Afterwards, of course, I'd shoot myself. Life wouldn't be worth living after that. ...

RICHARD

Oh, no!

(*A pause*)

Helen ...

HELEN

Yes?

RICHARD

Nothing. Nothing.

HELEN

Yes, there is something. I can tell.

RICHARD

No, now take it easy . . .

HELEN

I can tell. I can suddenly feel it. The vibrations—something happened while I was away this summer . . .

RICHARD

It was an accident. A crazy accident. There was this to-mato . . . That is—this tomato plant fell down. It landed right out there on the terrace. But nobody was hurt, thank God. I didn't want to tell you about it. I was afraid you'd worry. . . .

HELEN
(*Sadly*)

Who was she?

RICHARD

Now, Helen—you're making this up . . .

HELEN
(*Turning on him*)

Who was she!

RICHARD

Now please, really . . .

HELEN

Then it's true. It is true.

RICHARD

Look, we're both intelligent people. I knew you'd be hurt. But I know that somehow, some day, you'll forgive me. . . . (*He suddenly notices that* HELEN *is holding a revolver in her hand*) Now put that thing down. What are you going to do?

HELEN

You've left me nothing else to do. I'm going to shoot you dead. Then I'm going to kill myself.

RICHARD

But what about—the child?

HELEN

You should have thought of that before. Good-bye, Richard . . .

(*She fires five times.*)

(*For a moment,* RICHARD *stands erect, weathering the hail of bullets. . . . Then slowly, tragically, in the best gangster movie tradition—clutching his middle—and making small Bogart-like sounds he sinks to the floor.*)

RICHARD

(*Gasping—the beads of sweat standing out on his forehead*)

Helen—I'm—going—fast . . . Give me a cigarette. . . .

HELEN

(*Always the wife, even in times of crisis*)

A cigarette! You know what Dr. Murphy told you about smoking!

RICHARD

Good-bye . . . Helen . . .

(*She turns and walks sadly to the kitchen. At the door she stops, waves sadly with the wooden spoon, blows one final kiss and as the music swells she exits into kitchen. An instant later we hear the final shot.*

RICHARD *collapses in a final spasm of agony and the lights black out.*)

(*As the lights dim back to reality* RICHARD *is seated where we left him, a horror-struck expression on his face.*)

RICHARD

Oh, the hell with *that*! I'll be goddamned if I'll tell her! (*For a moment,* RICHARD *stands shaking his head*) But I've got to . . . I've just got to . . .

(*He is heading for the telephone when the sound of the door buzzer stops him.*)

(*He freezes, panic-stricken. Glances quickly at the bedroom. The buzzer sounds again. Then a third time.*)

(*When it is quite clear that whoever it is is not going to go away,* RICHARD *presses the buzzer, then opens the door a crack, still leaving the chain fastened.*)

RICHARD
(*Hoarsely*)

Who is it?

DR. BRUBAKER
(*Off stage*)

Once again, sir, I must trouble you . . .

RICHARD

Dr. Brubaker!

DR. BRUBAKER
(*Off stage*)

Yes . . .

RICHARD

What is it? What can I do for you?

DR. BRUBAKER
(*Through door*)
Last evening, after our conference, I appear to have left your apartment without my brief case.

RICHARD
No, no, Doctor. That's impossible. I'm afraid you're mistaken. I'm quite sure you had it with you. In fact, I remember quite clearly seeing ...

(*He looks wildly around the room and then sees the brief case*)

Oh. Oh, there it is. . . . You're right. Isn't that amazing? It's right there. I'm sorry I can't ask you in but the place is kind of a mess and ...

(*He is trying to get the brief case through the door without unfastening the chain. It doesn't fit. He attempts brute force, but it just isn't going to fit. He pounds at it wildly and then finally realizes that he is going to have to open the chain. He does so*)

Here you are, Doctor ... Good-bye ...

DR. BRUBAKER
(*An unstopable force, he moves into the living room*)
I thank you. If you will permit me, I'll just make sure that everything is in order ...

(*Opening the brief case and riffling through the contents*)

You can see what a strong unconscious resistance this whole project has stimulated in me. . . . I cannot understand this mass compulsion on the part of the psychiatric profession to write and publish books. . . .

RICHARD

Don't worry about it, Doctor. Books by psychiatrists almost always sell well. I'll talk to you again the first of the week. . . .

DR. BRUBAKER

Thank you, sir. And once again I must apologize for troubling you. Particularly in the midst of such a delicate situation . . .

RICHARD

Yes. Well . . . *What?* What do you mean? What delicate situation?

DR. BRUBAKER

I meant only that, as, quite clearly, your second assault on the person of the young lady was more successful than the first, my visit could not have been more inopportune. Good-bye, sir, and good luck!

(DR. BRUBAKER *starts to go.* RICHARD *stops him.*)

RICHARD

Now wait a minute, Doctor. Now wait a minute. You can't just say something like that and then go . . .

DR. BRUBAKER

My boy, I have a full day ahead of me. . . .

RICHARD

Look, I can't stand it. You've got to tell me. How did you know—about—what happened?

DR. BRUBAKER

In the light of our conversation of last evening, it is quite obvious. I return this morning to find you behind barred doors in an extreme state of sexomasochistic excitement bordering on hysteria. . . .

RICHARD

What the hell is sexomasochistic excitement?

DR. BRUBAKER

Guilt feelings, sir. Guilt feelings. A state of deep and utter enjoyment induced by reveling in one's guilt feelings. One punishes oneself and one is pardoned of one's crime. And now, my boy, I must really go. Enjoy yourself!

RICHARD

Look, this may not seem like very much to you—you spend eight hours a day with rapists and all kinds of—but I've never done anything like this before. . . .

DR. BRUBAKER

This is quite obvious.

RICHARD

This is the first time. And, by God, it's the last time. . . .

DR. BRUBAKER

An excellent decision.

RICHARD

I mean, I love my wife!

DR. BRUBAKER

Don't we all? And now, sir . . .

RICHARD

If she ever finds out about this she'll—kill us both. She'll kill *herself* anyway—and I don't want her to do that. Maybe it would be better if I didn't tell her. . . .

DR. BRUBAKER

Possibly . . .

RICHARD

But she'd find out some way. I know she would. What was that you said the other night? There was some phrase you used. What was it?

DR. BRUBAKER

(*He has wandered over to the bookshelf and taken down the copy of* US Camera)

Vigorous denial. This popular theory of the omniscience of wives is completely untrue. They almost never know. Because they don't want to.

RICHARD

Yeah. Yeah. Vigorous denial. Suppose I denied it. That's all. She'd have to take my word for it. As a matter of fact, you know, it's probably a damn good thing this happened. I mean, a couple of days ago—I wasn't even sure if I did love her. Now I know I do. Helen ought to be damn glad this happened, if you want to know ... (*He notices* DR. BRUBAKER *holding* US Camera) You can take that with you if you want to ...

DR. BRUBAKER

No. No, thank you.

RICHARD

You know, suddenly I feel much better. Everything's going to be all right. You're absolutely right, Doctor. I just won't tell her and everything'll be fine. And if she should find out, I'll deny it. . . .

DR. BRUBAKER

Vigorously.

RICHARD

Gee, Doctor—I'd like to give you fifty dollars or something ...

DR. BRUBAKER
(*Considers this briefly, but rejects it*)
Well . . . No, no. It will not be necessary . . .

(*He is casually thumbing through* US Camera *and stops at the* GIRL's *picture*)

However, if the young lady should by any chance suffer any severe traumatic or emotional disturbances due to your decision to go back to your wife . . . If, in other words, she appears to be in need of psychiatric aid—I trust you will mention my name. . . . Thank you once again, sir, and good day . . .

(*He hands* US Camera *back to* RICHARD *and exits.* RICHARD *looks after him thoughtfully for a moment or two. Then, the doors to the bedrooms slide open and* THE GIRL *emerges. She is dressed and is bright and cheerful and very much herself.*)

THE GIRL

Hi.

RICHARD

Oh. Hi.

THE GIRL

Golly, I didn't know it was so late. I don't know what happened to me. I've got to be at the studio in half an hour. . . .

RICHARD

The studio . . .

THE GIRL

Sure. The television show. Forty million people are waiting to see me wash my husband's shirt in Trill—that exciting new, no-rinse detergent . . .

RICHARD

Oh.

THE GIRL

Well, I'd better go now. . . .

RICHARD

I was going to make some coffee. . . .

THE GIRL

That's all right. I'll get some on the way.

RICHARD

I don't know how to say this—but you're . . . I mean, I . . .

THE GIRL

I know. Me too . . .

RICHARD

Will I see you—again, I mean?

THE GIRL

I think better not . . .

RICHARD

This whole thing—it's been swell. Only . . .

THE GIRL

Only one thing. We mustn't forget that . . .

RICHARD

What's that?

THE GIRL

This is your birthday.

RICHARD

Gee, that's right. It is.

THE GIRL

Well, I want this to be a happy birthday. . . .

RICHARD

Look. You're not upset about anything, are you?

THE GIRL

No. No, I feel fine. Are you?

RICHARD

Are you sure? I mean, well . . .

142

THE GIRL

No, really, I feel wonderful. . . . Only . . . Well, suddenly I feel like maybe it wouldn't be so bad to have to start getting in at one o'clock again. . . .

RICHARD

Didn't you say—I mean—wouldn't that spoil everything?

THE GIRL

You don't understand—I mean it would be pretty nice to have to start getting in at one o'clock again. As soon as I find someone who's fallen desperately in love with me—someone who's sweet and intelligent and married—to me . . . I don't mean you—I mean—you know—someone who . . .

RICHARD

Someone who never saw Sarah Bernhardt?

THE GIRL

Well, yes . . . Good-bye, and thanks for everything. . . . (*She kisses him lightly on the cheek*) Birthday kiss. Happy birthday, Richard.

RICHARD

Thank you . . .

(*She starts up the stairs then turns and stops.*)

THE GIRL

Hey—I forgot my hammer.

RICHARD

Yeah—you better take that ...

(*Both laugh and are released. She goes up the stairs. The trap closes and she is gone.*)
(RICHARD *is a little awed. In a dazed way he wanders over to the bar and pours himself a glass of milk. Then, he looks at his watch, pulls himself together, picks up* US Camera *and heads for bedroom. He puts* US Camera *on shelf, starts out. Comes back and drops it behind the row of books, hiding it. He starts out again and the door buzzer sounds. He goes to the door and opens it.* TOM MACKENZIE *is standing in the doorway.*)

TOM

Hi, there ...

RICHARD

Hello.

TOM

How are you? Hope I didn't wake you ...

RICHARD

What do you want?

TOM

I'm sorry to bust in on you at this ungodly hour, boy, but I'm here on business. Family business. Got any coffee?

RICHARD

No. What are you doing here? I thought you were up in the country.

TOM

I was. I just drove in this morning. Got an appointment with my agent so Helen asked me to stop by and ask you . . .

RICHARD

Oh! Oh, she did. Well, I'm damn glad she did. I want to talk to you.

TOM

What's the matter with you, boy? You're acting mighty peculiar.

RICHARD

Never mind how *I'm* acting. You think you're pretty fancy with your rain and your damn fireplaces . . .

TOM

What are you talking about? What fireplaces?

RICHARD

You know what fireplaces.

TOM

I don't even have a fireplace.

RICHARD

That's your story.

TOM

I put in radiant heat. It's the latest thing. Cost me three thousand dollars.

RICHARD

Oh, yeah?

TOM

Yeah! They take the coils and they bury them right in the floor. . . . What the hell is all this about fireplaces? Are you drunk or something?

RICHARD

No, I am not drunk! (*From above comes the sound of hammering, a nail being driven into the floor*) She had dinner with you last night, didn't she?

TOM

Sure. Sure. (*More hammering*) What's wrong with that?

RICHARD

And she was wearing that green dress from Clare Potter wasn't she?

TOM

How the hell do I know where she bought that green dress?

146

RICHARD

Oh, then she *was* wearing it! Worse than I thought!

TOM

You *are* drunk. (*More hammering. This time* TOM *looks up*) What's that?

RICHARD

That's nothing. This used to be a duplex. I just had a glass of milk!

TOM

(*Patiently*)

Now see here, old man. Why shouldn't Helen have dinner with me? She's stuck up there in the country while you're down here doing God knows what . . .

RICHARD

What do you mean by that?

TOM

I know what happens with guys like you when their wives are away. Don't forget, I used to be married myself.

RICHARD

I got a good mind to punch you right in the nose.

TOM

Why?

RICHARD

Why—because you're too old—that's why!

TOM

Too old—what are you talking about?

RICHARD

You're getting fat—you look like the portrait of Dorian Gray!

TOM

Drunk. Blind, stinking drunk at nine o'clock in the morning. Where am I getting fat?

RICHARD

Everywhere! You know, there's something really repulsive about old men who run after young wives! Now you get out of here and get back to Helen and tell her I refuse to give her a divorce. . . .

TOM

A divorce?

RICHARD

You heard me! You can tell her for me that I'll fight it in every court in the country!

TOM

You're crazy! Helen doesn't want a divorce. . . . (*Yelling, he can longer control himself*) She wants her yellow skirt!

148

RICHARD

Her yellow skirt? Oh, my God . . .

TOM
(*Bellowing*)
She's having people over for dinner and she needs it!
(*He exits slamming the door furiously.*)

RICHARD

Her yellow skirt . . .

(*He reaches into hall closet and finds it on the wire hanger. Tenderly, he folds it over his arm*)

I'll take her yellow skirt up to her myself. She needs it. She's having people over for dinner.
People over for dinner? *What* people?
Me! That's what people!

(*Takes his hat from closet, puts it on his head at a rakish angle and with a great flourish exits out the door as:*)

The curtain falls